CLASSIC TWOSOMES
for Girl and Boy Dolls

MARJORY FAINGES

Kangaroo Press

Acknowledgments

My sincere thanks go to all the marvellous doll people who have so willingly shared their copies of old knitting patterns, including the late Jane and Dorothy Coleman, USA; Carole Yocum, USA; Frances Baird and Phyllis Bamforth, England; Shirleyanne McKay, Anne Cochrane, Greta Gray, NSW; Ross Schmidt, WA; and especially to Jean Hardie and Joan Arkell who have helped by knitting copies of the required garments to prove the patterns. To the staff at Rabbit Photo, Stafford City, for their help and patience in achieving the effect I wanted with my photographs, and an extra special thanks to my very patient husband Jim, for all his help and encouragement, while writing and preparing the various pieces for this book.

CLASSIC TWOSOMES FOR GIRL AND BOY DOLLS

First published in Australia in 2001 by Kangaroo Press
an imprint of Simon & Schuster (Australia) Pty Limited
20 Barcoo Street, East Roseville NSW 2069

A Viacom Company
Sydney New York London Toronto Tokyo Singapore

National Library of Australia
Cataloguing-in-Publication data

Marjory Fainges, 1933–.

  Classic twosomes for girl and boy dolls.
  ISBN 0 7318 0924 6.

  1. Doll clothes - Patterns. I. Title.

745.5922

Set in 10/12 Times Roman by Asset Typesetting Pty Ltd
Printed in China by Everbest Printing Co.

10 9 8 7 6 5 4 3 2 1

Contents

Introduction

Many collectors may have two dolls that are practically the same, that they would like to dress as a matching pair, or even as twin dolls. This book is the ideal medium, with patterns that have been adjusted from old patterns, many of which were given as a set with designs to suit boy and girl dolls, thus making them twin dolls. Several lovely old patterns have led me, the author, into designing yet another pattern, sometimes for a boy doll, sometimes for a girl doll, to compliment the original pattern, thus making two outfits compatible to one another.

If taken separately, there are 24 patterns, 12 suitable for boy dolls, 12 suitable for girl dolls, and the patterns range in size to fit dolls from 18 cm (7 in) to 41–46 cm (16–18 in) depending on their waist measurements and the length of their legs.

As in my first book in this series, *Classic Knits for Boy Dolls*, I have chosen to present knitting patterns suitable for dolls from the late 1890s through to the late 1940s, and the late 1950s, by permission of Coats Patons. At the same time, because these are 'classic knits', they can be used on dolls of much later manufacture. I trust that in this book you will find just the pattern you have been looking for to recreate those wonderful remembered moments of long ago.
I hope you get as much enjoyment from knitting these garments as I have, both from researching, and making them. Some of your beautiful but difficult dolls can now be attired in a new suit of clothing, instead of sitting naked at the back of the cupboard, waiting for the day a pattern for a suitable outfit can be found. Happy knitting.

Proving old knitting patterns

As both the denier size or thickness of the wool ply, and the method of writing knitting pattern instructions, have changed greatly over the years, and as many of the old patterns had mistakes in them (such as the suitability of the pattern to the number of stitches required, or lines of pattern omitted), I have had to prove every one of the patterns in this book before passing them on to my friend Joan Arkell, who kindly and willingly knitted and recorded either smaller or larger versions of many of the patterns.

Changing the look, but keeping to the basic pattern

In several of the patterns included in this book, it can be shown that by simply changing either the number of rows of colour in a stripe pattern or the number of colours used in a checkered pattern, many combinations and variations can be achieved with just a little thought.

As in all my knitting books so far published, by simply changing the needles and the ply of the wool when knitting one of the outfits shown in each category, the outfits then become excellent for different sized dolls or different aged dolls, and by doing this the dolls become brother and sister dolls.

Altering the size of a pattern

The outfits included here will fit dolls ranging in size from 12.5 cm (5 in) to 56 cm (22 in). Using a combination of garments from different patterns will give an even greater variety. Other outfits are portrayed on dolls that may be of a different size, shape and period, and it is here that my instructions differ from the norm; instead of giving the number of stitches required for a bigger size, I have for simplicity used the difference that a variation in ply and size of needles can give to produce the required sizes for different dolls. Thus with no extra effort, following the examples given in these instructions, clothing for larger or smaller dolls can be made from any of the patterns given, just by adjusting the size of the needles and the wool or yarn used.

If you like a pattern which is too small for your particular doll, you can change to 5-ply wool and bigger needles, such as 4.0 or 4.5 mm (8 or 7) [US 6 or 7], or even larger sized wool and needles. The garment will end up much bigger than the original, without having to change the number of stitches and rows. On the other hand, knitting a pattern with 1.0 mm (16) or finer needles and very fine wool or yarn, down to 1-ply, will give you much smaller finished garments.

For this reason the instructions for the patterns are all given in rows, rather than measured in centimetres or inches. As long as you remember to change the wool or yarn size in proportion with the needle size, the garments will remain in true proportion.

Tension

As some knitters work more loosely (or more tightly) than others, I suggest that you work a trial piece of knitting, 10 sts by 10 rows, to see if your tension is the same as that recommended in the pattern.

If your sample has more stitches or rows than in the pattern, use needles a size smaller; use needles a size larger if your sample has less stitches or rows. If you are an uneven knitter here is a little hint - work your purl rows using a size larger needle than in your knit rows - it works.

Needle sizes

All instructions are given in both metric and imperial measurements, with Australian, English and US sizes of knitting needles or crochet hooks specified.

Wool or other suitable yarns?

I have used woollen yarn where possible throughout the book, mainly because wool was the medium used in the original patterns. For many of the patterns I have used Bendigo 2-ply and 3-ply fingering wool, which are both available in quite a wide range of both subdued and vibrant colours.

This wool is easily available by mail order direct from the Bendigo Woollen Mills in Bendigo, Victoria (they take most credit cards also). Customers from the USA can order direct via a toll-free phone number (see page 48); other overseas customers can reach them by mail or fax. For other patterns I have used Patons 3-ply Baby Wool or 4-ply Patonyle, both because Coats Patons have kindly given me permission to use patterns from knitting books they have published, and also because these wools are readily available.

In the patterns that I have designed myself I have used both makes of wool to show the versatility of what can be achieved.

Other wools or yarns, such as those based on nylon, can readily be used. My only suggestion is that you start by making the smallest garment in an outfit to check what difference in size, if any, the different yarn may produce.

Knitting terminology

A very important side to knitting is knowing what all the different terms and abbreviations mean. These are covered fully on page 10. For American knitters I have included a small but concise translation of the differences in crochet terminology because simple crochet is used for the finish of some of the garments.

Garment size and your doll

The sizes of the actual garments are given in both metric and imperial measurements, so all you have to do is measure your doll in the appropriate places, regardless of its age, to see whether the garment you have chosen will fit using the materials given. You may have to change the size of wool and needles, always remembering that *knitted clothes stretch,* and thus can fit a doll bigger than the actual measurements given.

Choosing appropriate patterns

Where possible in the photographs I have used dolls of an age in keeping with the age of the original patterns, but I have also shown more modern dolls wearing the same outfits. As all these patterns are classic in style they can really be used on dolls of any age, ranging in size from 12.5 cm (5 in) to 56 cm (22 in).

Finishing the garment

To press or not? Pressing is a very important part of giving the finished garment a professional look. If you have used pure woollen yarn, gently press (not iron) each piece of the garment before sewing up, using either a steam iron at a low steam temperature, or a medium heat dry iron on a slightly damp cloth placed over the garment piece.

Do not heat-press any garment made from nylon or bri-nylon yarn.

How to Knit

(*or* Knitting for Beginners, *courtesy of Patons Woolcraft*)

Casting-on—making the first loop

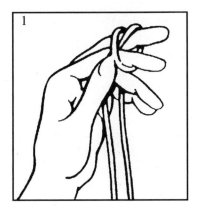 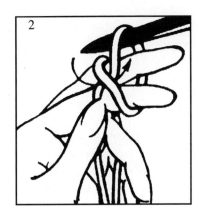 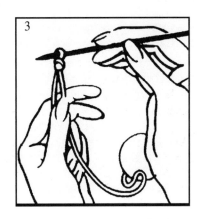

1. Wrap the yarn around the first and second fingers of the left hand.
2. Place point of needle under the front loop and draw back loop through.
3. Withdraw fingers from loop and draw loop up onto needle

Casting-on using thumb and one needle

4. Using the thumb and one needle, and working with a length of yarn sufficient for the required number of sts in your left hand, pass the yarn around the left thumb.
5. Place point of needle beneath loop on the thumb, drawing loop up slightly.

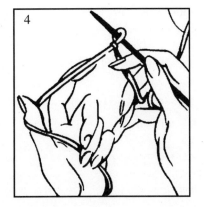 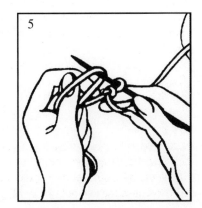

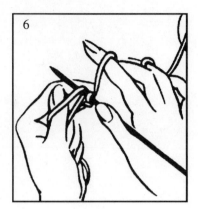

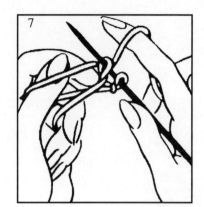

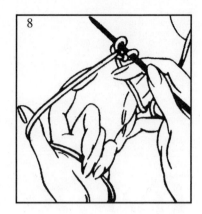

6. Hold yarn from ball in right hand ready to pass around the point of the needle.
7. Wrap yarn from ball around the point of the needle and draw through loop on thumb.
8. Draw up stitch on needle, pull both ends of yarn firmly, and repeat from step 1 until sufficient stitches have been cast on.

Points to watch:
- An even cast-on is essential to good knitting
- Avoid casting-on too tightly, as edge will not hang properly.
- This form of casting-on does not necessitate knitting into the back of the cast-on stitches.
- This method can be used for all general purposes.

Casting-on using two needles

Make a loop (following diagrams 1 to 3), then place the point of the right-hand needle through the loop on the left-hand needle. Holding the yarn in the right hand, wrap the yarn around the point of the right-hand needle and draw the yarn through the loop on the left-hand needle, forming a second loop. Place this loop onto the left-hand needle (diagram 9). Now place the point of the right-hand needle *between the two loops on the left-hand needle.* Wrap the yarn around the end of the right-hand needle (diagram 10) and draw a loop between the two loops on the left-hand needle. Place this loop onto the left-hand needle. Put the point of the right-hand needle between the first and second loops on the left-hand needle (counting from the point). Repeat until required number of stitches has been cast on.

Points to watch:
Keep the stitches on the left-hand needle near the point. The yarn should come *over* the first finger of the right hand, *under* the second, *over* the third and *under* the fourth. The yarn should pass easily through the fingers, but should be held firmly to maintain an even tension.

Knitting a stitch

Hold the needle containing the cast-on stitches in the left hand. Insert the right needle from left to right through the first loop, pass the yarn around the point of the right-hand needle, draw a new loop through and, retaining this loop on the right-hand needle, slip the first loop off the left-hand needle (diagram 11).

In plain knitting the wool or yarn is always held at the back of the work. More than one row of knitting stitch creates the pattern known as garter stitch (diagram 12).

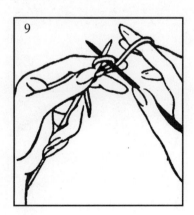

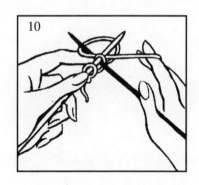

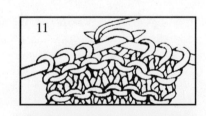

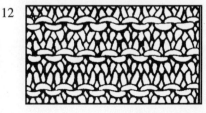

Purling a stitch

Holding the yarn or wool to the front of the work (this is essential when purling), insert the right-hand needle from right to left through the first loop on the left-hand needle, pass the yarn around the point of the right-hand needle, draw the loop so formed through stitch onto right-hand needle and drop stitch off left-hand needle. Repeat this action across row (diagram 13).

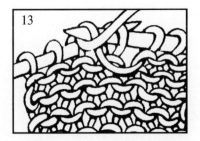

Stocking stitch

By knitting one row and purling the next row a plain smooth pattern is created-this is known as stocking stitch or st st. The side facing you when you work the knit row is usually the right side of the work. Thus the purl side will be the wrong side (unless otherwise stated in the pattern). See diagram 14.

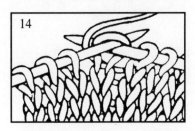

Casting off

Knit the first two stitches, *insert the point of the left-hand needle from left to right through the first of these two stitches, slip this stitch over the second one, that is, take it off the right-hand needle, thus leaving one stitch on the right-hand needle (diagram 15).

Knit the next stitch and repeat from * until only one loop remains. Break off the yarn and draw the end through the loop of the last stitch. Thread yarn through a yarn needle and darn it neatly into the work.

Important Unless otherwise stated, the edge formed by the cast-off stitches should be as elastic as the remainder of the garment.

When casting off at the beginning of a row (e.g. at the armholes) remember that if 6 sts are cast off, for example, 7 will be needed and used in order to cast off the 6th. This 7th st, therefore, has not been disposed of and must be included in the number of stitches left on the row, and must be counted as the first of such stitches.

Tension

The simplest method of measuring tension is to cast on 20 sts using the size of needle and the yarn specified in the pattern (over smooth fabric), knit a square and press lightly. Check the tension by placing a measuring tape along the stitches, marking 2.5 cm (1 in) with pins and counting the exact number of stitches within the measured length.

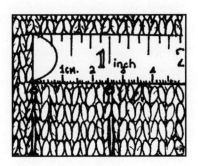

Useful Information

Wool thicknesses

Australian	American
2-ply	2-ply fingering
3-ply	3-ply fingering
4-ply	4-ply fingering
5-ply	

Knitting needle sizes

Metric (mm)	Imperial	American
2.0	14	0
2.5	13–12	1
3.0	11	2–3
3.5	10	4
3.75	9	5
4.0	8	6
4.5	7	7
5.0	6	8
5.5	5	9
6.0	4	10
6.5	3	—
7.0	2	11
7.5	1	—

Crochet hooks

Metric (mm)	Imperial	American
2.0	14	B/1
2.5	12	C/2
3.0	10	D/3
3.5	9	E/4
4.0	8	F/5
4.5	7	G/6
5.0	6	H/8
5.5	5	I/9
6.0	4	J/10
7.0	2	—

Abbreviations and terminology

* *	repeat instructions between * *
****	refer back to previous section of pattern
alt	alternate
beg	beginning
C	contrast, or lesser colour used in two-colour knitting
dec	decrease—work 2 sts tog to form 1 st
g	gram/s
garter st	work every row in knit stitch
inc	work twice into st to make 2 sts
in	inch(es)
k	knit
m1	make a stitch by placing wool over needle before the next st
MC	main colour used in two-colour knitting
mm	millimetre
ms	moss stitch—work k1, p1, alternately in following rows to give a broken rib effect; usually worked on an uneven no. of stitches
no.	number
oz	ounce/s
p	purl
psso	pass the slipped stitch over
rep	repeat
rib	usually either k1, p1, or k2, p2, normally worked on an even no. of stitches, repeated to end of row
rib	in the case of garter st, the number of raised rows showing on one side of knitting
sl or sl st	slip the stitch onto needle
st/s	stitch/es
st st	stocking st—working one row in knit st and following row in purl st
tbl	through back loop
tog	working 2 sts together to form 1 st
turn	reverse the way of knitting by working back on the needle just worked
wl fwd	bringing wool to front of work, before working next st, thus making a st; used in patterns and for small buttonholes
wrn	wool round needle

Handy hints

1. Knit through back of stitch on all cast-on stitches, using the two-needle method, to give a firm edge, particularly when this method has been used for making a buttonhole.
2. When picking up a stitch, pick up and knit before transferring it onto other needle.

Equivalent crochet terms

Australian/European		*American*
ch (chain)	=	ch (chain)
sl st (single crochet)	=	sl st (slip st)
dc (double crochet)	=	sc (single crochet)
tr (treble)	=	dc (double crochet)

Old knitting books

Some Australian readers may have old Patons knitting books which include patterns for doll's clothes. Coats Patons have supplied the years of publication but advise that these books are now *out of print*, and cannot be obtained from the company or its outlets.

Book No. C.3	Published before 1950, reprinted 1950
C.4	Reprinted 1954
C.5	Published 1953, reprinted 1955
C.8	Published 1955, reprinted 1957
C.12	Published 1958
C.13	Published 1959
C.14	Published 1960
C.18	Published 1963
C.23	Published 1970
C.26	Published 1971
C.28	Published 1972
C.38	Published 1979

Care of woollen garments

It takes only a little effort to give knitted garments the care they deserve, especially those made of natural fibres such as pure wool. Make the care regular and you will be rewarded with fresh, new looking clothes for a lifetime.

2-ply, 3-ply and 4-ply wool fingering, and other pure woollen yarns
Warm hand wash only in approved detergent.
Do not rub.
Do not bleach.
Warm rinse well—rinsing is essential.
Normal spin.
Do not tumble dry.
Dry flat and protect from direct sunlight.
Warm iron.
If drycleaning is required, P.50°C is the highest temperature needed.

Baby wool
Read the instructions as many baby wools are now machine washable.
Warm machine wash, short gentle cycle in approved detergent.
Do not rub.
Do not bleach.
Warm rinse well—rinsing is essential
Normal spin.
Do not tumble dry.
Dry flat—protect from direct sunlight.
Warm iron.
(Instructions courtesy Bendigo Woollen Mills.)

Antoinette and Anthony

Based on a 1937 pattern intended for 30 cm (12 in) dolls with papier-mâché heads and cloth bodies, the two outfits would look equally at home on jointed bisque headed dolls of the same size (with thin bodies) or even some of the thin bodied plastic dolls of today.

Materials (will make both outfits)
50 g (2 oz) 4-ply wool in MC
50 g (2 oz) 4-ply wool in W
1 pair 3.75 mm (9) (US 5) knitting needles
3 mm (11) (D) crochet hook
2 small buttons
2 small snap fasteners or tiny buttons
Length of thin elastic

Measurements

Anthony

Short Pants

Waist to crutch	7 cm	(2¾ in)
Side seam	9 cm	(3½ in)
Leg seam	2.5 cm	(1 in)
Waist	18 cm	(7 in)

Jumper

Shoulder to hem	11.5 cm	(4½ in)
Width around chest	19 cm	(3¾)
Side seam	6.5 cm	(2½ in)
Sleeve seam	6 cm	(2¼ in)

Antoinette

Dress

Shoulder to hem	18 cm	(7 in)
Shoulder to dropped waist	10.5 cm	(4¼ in)
Length of skirt	7.5 cm	(3 in)
Side seam	13.5 cm	(5¼ in)
Width around chest	18 cm	(7 in)
Sleeve seam	6 cm	(2½ in)

Belt 21.5 cm (8½ in)

Panties

Around waist	18 cm	(7 in)
Waist to crutch	7.5 cm	(3 in)
Side seam	5 cm	(2 in)

Tension
6 sts = 2.50 cm (1 in)

Anthony's short pants

With 3.75 mm (9) (US 5) needles and MC, cast on 12 sts and work in st st for 8 rows, then break off wool and work another leg in the same manner.
Working across all 24 sts, work 18 rows in st st starting with a knit row.
Work in k1, p1 rib for 3 rows.
Slots for elastic   k1, *(wl fwd, k2 tog) rep from * to last st, p1.
Work 2 rows in k1, p1 rib.
Cast off.
Work another side the same way.

To make up
Sew up the side and leg seams and insert elastic through holes to fit waist.

Anthony's pullover (sweater)

Back and front alike
With 3.75 mm (9) (US 5) needles and MC, cast on 27 sts and knit 1 row into the back of the cast on sts.

Commence pattern
1st row   Leaving the MC hanging, and using W only *p1, sl 1 purlwise, rep from * to last st, p1.
2nd row   *k1, sl 1 knitwise, rep from * to last st, k1.
3rd row   Leaving W hanging, use MC and purl the row.
4th row   Knit in MC.
Rep the last 4 rows 7 times, then continue in pattern, dec at each end of next 4 rows.
Work 8 rows in pattern.
Next row   Work 5 sts in pattern, cast off 9 sts, work 5 sts in pattern.

Work 7 rows in pattern on these last 5 sts. Cast off.
Join wool at neck edge for other side, and work 7 rows in pattern. Cast off.
Work another side to match.

Sleeves

With 3.75 mm (9) (US 5) needles and MC, cast on 19 sts and with the MC, and then the W, work in pattern as for the pullover (sweater) for 7 patterns, then dec at each end of every row until 7 sts remain. Cast off.
Work another sleeve to match.

To make up

Sew up side seams and insert sleeves, leaving one shoulder seam unsewn. Using MC, work 2 rows of double crochet (US sc) around neck and across shoulder. Fasten shoulder with tiny snap fasteners.

Antoinette's panties

With 3.75 mm (9) (US 5) needles and W, cast on 24 sts, and work in k1, p1 rib pattern for 2 rows.
Next row   K1, *wl fwd, k2 tog, rep from * to last st, p1.
Work 3 rows in k1, p1 rib.
Work 10 rows in st st.
Dec at each end of every row until 6 sts remain. Cast off.
Work another side to match.

To make up

Sew up side seams and between legs. Insert elastic to fit waist.

Antoinette's frock

With 3.75 mm (9) (US 5) knitting needles and MC, cast on 45 sts.
Knit into the back of the cast on sts.
1st row   *k3, p3, rep to last 3 sts, k3.
2nd row   *p3, k3, rep to last 3 sts, p3.
Rep the last 2 rows twice.
7th row   *k2 tog, k1, p3, rep from * to last 3 sts, k1, k2 tog.
8th row   *p2, k3, rep from * to last 2 sts, p2.
9th row   *k2, p3, rep from * to last 2 sts, k2.
Rep the last two rows twice, then the 8th row once.
15th row   *k2 tog, p3, rep from * to the last 2 sts, k2 tog.
16th row   *p1, k3, rep from * to last st, p1.
17th row   *k1, p3, rep from * to last st, k1.
Rep the last 2 rows three times.
Next row   k2 tog, work in pattern to last 2 sts, k2 tog.
Leave MC hanging.

Bodice

Join in W and work pattern as follows.
1st row   Purl.
2nd row   Knit, leave W hanging.
3rd row   With MC, *p1, sl 1 purlwise, rep from * to last st, p1.
4th row   *k1, sl 1 knitwise, rep from * to last st, k1. Leave MC hanging.
Rep the last 4 pattern rows 7 times.
Dec 1 st at each end of needle in next 4 rows.
Work 8 rows in pattern.
Next row   Work 5 sts in pattern, cast off 9 sts, work 5 sts in pattern.
On last 5 sts, work 7 rows in pattern. Cast off.
Return to neck edge and on remaining 5 sts, work 7 rows in pattern. Cast off.
Work other side to match.

Sleeves

With 3.75 mm (9) (US 5) needles and W, cast on 19 sts, and with W and then MC, work in pattern as given for bodice, for 7 patterns, then dec at each end of every row until 7 sts remain. Cast off.
Work another sleeve to match.

To make up

Sew up one shoulder seam, and sew the other shoulder seam only at the sleeve end. Insert sleeves and sew up sleeve seams and side seams. Work 2 rows of dc (US sc) around neck and across open shoulder.
Sew tiny snap fasteners on open shoulder seam.

Belt

With 3.75 mm (9) (US 5) needles and MC, cast on 6 sts.
Work in k1, p1 rib for 18 cm (7 in). Cast off.
Sew a pearl button on each end and make a loop at one end of belt to fasten around button.

Benny and Jenny

Based on a early pattern by Patons, and worked in garter stitch throughout, these easy-to-make sets of versatile garments fit the popular 36 cm (14 in) dolls. The garments are not only suitable for twin (or brother and sister) dolls, but they can also be used as mix-and-match outfits. By using two contasting or toning colours, the jackets and hats are easily interchangeable, giving even more outfits.

Materials
75 g (3 oz) 5-ply wool in MC (will make the two sets)
75 g (3 oz) 5-ply wool in C (will make the two sets)
small amount of 5-ply wool in W for Jenny's panties
1 pair 3.75 mm (9) (US 5) knitting needles
3.00 mm (11) (US 3/D) crochet hook
Length of elastic

Measurements
Remember: garter st stretches

Benny

Jacket

Shoulder to hem	10 cm	(4 in)
Side seam	6 cm	(2½ in)
Width around at hem	27 cm	(10½ in)
Width at chest (double-breasted)	23 cm	(9 in)
Width at chest (single-breasted)	25 cm	(10 in)
Sleeve seam	9 cm	(3½ in)

Long trousers

Waist to crutch	7.5 cm	(3 in)
Inside leg	12.5 cm	(5 in)
Outside leg seam	20 cm	(8 in)
Waist	18 cm	(7 in)

Cap

Crown to brim	10 cm	(4 in)
Crown to turnback brim	7.5 cm	(3 in)
Width around brim	23 cm	(9 in)

Jenny

Jacket

Shoulder to hem	10 cm	(4 in)
Side seam	6 cm	(2½ in)
Width around at hem	27 cm	(10½ in)
Width at chest (double breasted)	23 cm	(9 in)
Width at chest (single breasted)	25 cm	(10 in)
Sleeve seam	9 cm	(3½ in)

Skirt

Waist to hem	10 cm	(4 in)
Waist (ungathered)	25 cm	(10 in)
Width around hem	36.5 cm	(14½ in)

Hat

Crown to front brim	9.5 cm	(3¾ in)
Crown to front edge (turnback brim)	7.5 cm	(3 in)
Width around brim	23 cm	(9 in)

Panties

Waist to crutch	9.5 cm	(3¾ in)
Width around waist	21 cm	(8¼ in)
Side seam	7 cm	(2¾ in)

Tension
6 rows   = 2.5 cm (1 in)
6 stitches = 2.5 cm (1 in)

Jenny's jacket

Main part of jacket is worked in one piece.
Starting at the base of the back, with 3.75 mm (9) (US 5) needles and C, cast on 28 sts.
Work 46 rows in garter st (23 ridges).
Divide for neck as follows.
Next row   k10. Place these 10 sts on a safety knitting pin. Cast off 8 sts, knit to end of the row.
Work 5 rows garter st on the remaining 10 sts.
At neck edge, cast on 8 sts for the revers.
Knit 45 rows in garter st. Cast off.
Slip the remaining 10 sts off the safety pin onto your needle (making sure the point of the needle is at the neck edge.
Work 6 rows in garter st.
Cast on 8 sts at the neck edge, and work 45 rows in garter st. Cast off.

Sleeves
With 3.75 mm (9) (US 5) needles and C, cast on 22 sts.
Knit 40 rows. Cast off.
Knit another sleeve the same.

To make up

Place a pin just above the 15th ridge on both sides of the back and at the sides of both fronts. This is the beginning of the armhole. Pin the cast off edge of the sleeve in position between the pins and sew in place. Sew up the side seams and the sleeve seams.

With dark colour and using a 3.00 mm (11) (C-D) crochet hook, work a row of dc (US sc) around the edge of the front and back edges, and the ends of both sleeves. Turn back the revers at both fronts, and tack in place with a couple of stitches in the light colour. Depending on the length of the doll's arms, you may turn back the cuffs of the sleeves. Place jacket on doll, and mark where the 4 buttons are to go- remembering that this is mainly a double-breasted jacket, but if the doll is a little on the chubby side, it can be a single-breasted jacket. Sew two small buttons on the right side of the jacket and two on the left side of the jacket (these two can be gently pushed through between the stitches thus forming buttonholes).

Jenny's skirt

Worked in one piece.
With 3.75 mm (9) (US 5) needles and C, cast on 96 sts.
Work 6 rows of garter st in C, change to MC.

Stripe pattern
Work 2 rows of garter st in MC, 2 rows of garter st in C, 2 rows of garter st in MC, break off MC.
Work 24 rows of garter st in C.
Next row   *k10, k2 tog, rep from * to end of row.
Work 3 rows in garter st.
Next row   *k 9, K2 tog, rep from * to end of row.
Work 3 rows in garter st.
Next row   k3, k2 tog, rep from * to end of row.
Work 1 row in garter st.
Next row   *k1, m1, k2 tog, rep from * to end of row.
Knit 2 rows in garter st. Cast off.

To make up
Join up back seam, and thread elastic through holes at waist to suit measurement of doll.

Jenny's hat (cap)

With 3.75 mm (9) (US 5) needles and C, cast on 52 sts.
Work 4 rows of garter st in C.
Work stripe pattern as follows: 2 rows of MC, 2 rows of C, 2 rows of MC, break off MC.
Work 16 rows in C.
Next row   *k11, k2 tog, rep from * to end of row.

Knit 3 rows.
Next row   *k10, k2 tog, rep from * to end of row.
Knit 3 rows.
Next row   *k9, k2 tog, rep from * to end of row.
Knit 1 row.
Next row   *k8, k2 tog, rep from * to end of row.
Knit 1 row.
Next row   *k7, k2 tog, rep from * to end of row.
Knit 1 row.
Next row   *k1, k2 tog, rep from * to last st, k1.

To make up
Break off wool leaving a long length. Thread through a darning needle. With thread double, pass darning needle through sts on needle. Pull wool tight to draw sts together, and fasten off with several sts. Sew up seam of hat from back to where you started decreases. Turn back stripe pattern to form brim of hat, and attach light coloured ribbons to each side to tie hat with. If you want it to be a cap, sew entire seam and then turn back stripe pattern to form turn back of cap.

Jenny's panties

With 3.75 mm (9) (US 5) needles and W, cast on 25 sts.
Work 2 rows in k1, p1 rib.
Next row   k1, *wl fwd, k2 tog rep from * to end.
Work 2 rows in k1, p1 rib.
Work 15 rows in st st, starting with a purl row.
Dec 1 st at each end of needle until 5 sts remain.
Work 2 rows. Cast off.
Make another piece the same.

To make up
Sew up cast-off edges and side seams. Thread elastic through waist.

Benny's jacket

Back and front worked in one piece.
With 3.75 mm (9) (US 5) needles and MC, cast on 28 sts.
Work 4 rows in garter st, join in C.
Stripe pattern   Work 2 rows of C, 2 rows of MC, 2 rows of C, break off C.
With MC, work 36 rows in garter st.
Next row   k10, cast off 8, k10.
Work 5 rows on the last 10 sts.
Next row   (neck edge) Cast on 8 sts for revers and knit 36 rows, finishing so the next row is on the right side of work. Join in C.
Work stripe pattern of 2 rows of C, 2 rows of MC, 2 rows of C. Break off C.

Work 4 rows in MC. Cast off.
Return to neck edge and work 6 rows of garter st on the remaining 10 sts.

Next row   Cast on 8 sts.
Work 35 rows of garter st, making sure your next row will be on the right side of work, join in light colour.

Stripe pattern   In garter st, work 2 rows of C, 2 rows of MC, 2 rows of C. Break off C.
Work 4 rows in garter st. Cast off.

Sleeves
With 3.75 mm (9) (US 5) needles and MC, cast on 22 sts.
Knit 40 rows. Cast off.
Work another sleeve the same.

To make up
Count up 10 ridges from stripe pattern on seam edge of back and fronts, and mark with a pin. Place sleeves between these markers and sew into position. Sew up side seams and sleeve seams. For Benny, fold left side of front over right and mark where buttons come. Sew buttons in place, and work buttons through knitting to work as buttonholes. If needed, catch revers back with a couple of stitches in matching wool.

Benny's trousers

With 3.75 mm (9) (US 5) needles and MC, cast on 24 sts.
Knit 2 rows in garter st.
Holes for elastic   *k1, m1, k2 tog, rep from * to end of row.
Work 88 rows in garter st (44 ridges). Cast off.
Work another leg the same.

To make up
Starting from the waist, join front and back seams from top to 28 rows (14 ridges) from hole row.
Sew up leg seams (60 rows) (30 ridges). If legs are too long, turn back bottom as cuffs.

Benny's cap

With 3.75 mm (9) (US 5) needles and MC, cast on 52 sts.
Work 4 rows in garter st, join in C.
Stripe pattern   In garter st work 2 rows of C, 2 rows of MC, 2 rows of C, break off MC.
Work 34 rows in MC.
Break off wool, leaving a long end.

To make up
Thread end double through a darning needle and pass darning needle through the centre of stitches on your knitting needle. Carefully pull wool tight so that all stitches are drawn close together. Fasten off securely, then sew up side seam. Turn back stripe pattern to finish off cap.

PATTERN ON PAGE 12

'Giddy-up,' says Anthony, a 30 cm (12 in) papier-mâché shoulderplate head on a cloth body, as he urges on an early 'Elasolin' set of horses and limber. Standing by his side in her matching 4-ply outfit is Antoinette, a similar 30 cm (12 in) German cloth doll with papier-mâché shoulderplate head.

PATTERN ON PAGE 14

'See, it works like this,' says Benny, a 36 cm (14 in) jointed German composition doll, dressed in his new knitted garter stitch suit. He shows off his German made *Marklin* railway crane to Jenny who is tightly clutching her all bisque little girl doll. Jenny, dressed in her simple to make 5-ply garter stitch knitted suit, is a 36 cm (14 in) 'Bright Eyes', fully composition doll by Horsman USA.

PATTERN ON PAGE 17

'No! You can't have my rocking horse,' says Cecilia, a 25 cm (10 in) Australian hard plastic
'Patsy' baby doll, as it is eyed off by Cecil, a 25 cm (10 in) Australian hard plastic Cherub
baby doll. Both dolls are dressed in their matching 3-ply, going-out winter outfits, which are decorated
with a contrasting stripe motif.

The sun is shining, so Cecilia has taken off her short jacket and pixie bonnet. She sits with Claude a
30 cm (12 in) Australian hard plastic baby doll by Moldex, as he displays the matching boy's summer
outfit of short pants and short-sleeved jumper.

PATTERN ON PAGE 22

'Down they go,' says Darryl, as he helps his sister Meryl play with their miniature diecast metal Playground Set by D.C.M.T. England. Dressed in matching 5-ply outfits are Darryl, a 41 cm (16 in) Australian hard plastic Cherub walking doll, and Meryl, a 41 cm (16 in) Australian hard plastic 'Patsy' baby doll.

Cecil and Cecilia

This wonderful set of clothes for your favourite 23–28 cm (9½–11 in) dolls, includes a lovely little dress, short jacket and pixie hood with contrast accents, plus panties for the girl doll, and a pram set of jacket and leggings (for winter) along with a bordered jumper and short pants for the boy doll. What more could your favourite dolls wish for.

Materials

50 g (2 oz) 3-ply baby wool in MC for Cecilia's jacket, dress, pixie hood and panties
50 g (2 oz) 3-ply baby wool in MC for Cecil's jacket, beret, leggings and jumper (If only making the jacket, beret and leggings, 25 g (1 oz) will be enough.)
25 g (1 oz) 3-ply baby wool in C for Cecil's short pants (optional) and outfit
25 g (1 oz) 3-ply baby wool in C for Cecilia's outfit
1 pair of 3.00 mm (11) (US 2–3) knitting needles
6 small buttons (for the two sets)
A length of elastic for the pants

Measurements

Cecil

Jacket

Shoulder to hem	11 cm	(4½ in)
Armhole to hem	7.5 cm	(3 in)
Width around hem	29cm	(11½ in)
Sleeve seam	5.5 cm	(2¼ in)

Leggings

Waist to crutch	8 cm	(3 in)
Around waist	20 cm	(8 in)
Inside leg to toe	12 cm	(4¾ in)
Outside leg to toe	17 cm	(6¾ in)

Beret

Circumference	18 cm	(7 in)
Hem to crown	7.5 cm	(3 in)

Jumper

Shoulder to hem	10 cm	(4 in)
Width around chest	21 cm	(8¼ in)
Side seam	6.5 cm	(2½ in)
Sleeve seam	2 cm	(¾ in)

Short pants

Waist to crutch	8.5 cm	(3½ in)
Width around waist	19 cm	(7½ in)
Side seam	7 cm	(2¾ in)

Cecilia

Jacket

Shoulder to hem	10 cm	(4 in)
Armhole to hem	6 cm	(2½ in)
Width around hem	29 cm	(11½ in)
Sleeve seam	5.5 cm	(2¼ in)

Dress

Shoulder to hem	16.5 cm	(6½ in)
Armhole to hem	12 cm	(4¾ in)
Width around chest at a/hole	22.5 cm	(9 in)
Width around at hem	46 cm	(18 in)
Sleeve seam	3 cm	(1¼ in)

Pixie hood

Brim to back point	10.5 cm	(4¼ in)
Brim to back of neck	7 cm	(2¾ in)
Width around brim	17 cm	(6¾ in)

Panties

Waist to crutch	8 cm	(3¼ in)
Width around waist	18 cm	(7 in)
Side seam	4.5 cm	(1¾ in)

Tension

8 st = 2.5 cm (1 in)

Cecil's jacket

Worked in one piece to the armholes.
With 3.00 mm (11) (US 2–3) needles and MC, cast on 93 sts. Work 4 rows in ms.
1st row ms6, knit to the last 8 sts, k2 tog starting with a purl, ms to end of row (92 sts).
2nd row ms6 sts, purl to last 6 sts, starting with 1p, ms to end of row.
3rd row ms6, knit to last 6 sts, ms6 sts.
4th row As 2nd row.
5th row ms6 MC, join in C and *k2 C, k2 MC, rep from * to last 6 sts, ms to end in MC.

6th row ms6 MC, *p2 C, 2 MC, rep from * to last 6 sts, ms to end in MC.

Rep the 5th and 6th rows once. Break of C.

Rep the 3rd and 4th rows 5 times (waistline).

Dec row ms6, *k1, k2 tog, rep from * until 8 sts remain, k2, ms6 (66 sts).

Next row As 4th row.

Rep the 3rd and 4th rows 3 times.

To shape armholes

Next row ms6, k12, cast off 4 sts, k22 (counting st on needle), cast off 4 sts, knit to end of row.

Left front

On the last 18 sts, work as follows:

1st row ms6, p12.

2nd row k12, ms6.

Rep the last 2 rows 4 times.

** To shape the neck

Cast off 7 sts, purl to end.

Continue working in st st and dec 1 st at the neck edge on every alternate row until 8 sts remain. Cast off.

Back

With wrong side facing, join in MC to the centre 22 sts. Beginning with a purl row, work 13 rows in st st

To slope the shoulders

Cast off 8 sts at the beginning of the next 2 rows, then cast off remaining sts.

Right front

With wrong side facing join in wool to the remaining 18 sts, and work as follows:

1st row p12, ms6.

2nd row ms6, k12.

Rep the last 2 rows 3 times and then the first row again, then rep the neck shaping from ** on the left front to the end.

Sleeves

Beginning at the wrist edge and using 3.00 mm (11) (US 2–3) needles and MC, cast on 24 sts.

Work 4 rows in ms.

Work 2 rows in st st, then inc 1 st at both ends of the next row and in every following 4th row until the 4th inc row has been worked, finishing on a knit row (32 sts).

Purl 1 row.

To shape sleeve top

Dec 1 st at both ends of the next 12 rows. Cast off remaining 8 sts.

Work a second sleeve in the same way.

Collar

With 3.00 mm (11) (US 2–3) needles and MC, cast on 52 sts. Work 2 rows in ms then work as follows:

1st row ms4, k44, m4.

2nd row ms4, p44, ms4.

3rd row ms4, join in C, *k2 C, k2 MC, rep from * to last 4 sts, ms4 MC.

4th row ms4 MC, *p2 C, p2 MC, rep from * to last 4 sts, ms4 MC. Break off C.

5th row ms4, knit to last 4 sts, ms4.

6th row ms4, p9, *p2 tog, p6, rep from * until 15 sts remain, p2 tog, p9, ms4.

Cast off.

To make up

Join shoulder seams, set sleeves into armholes join sleeve seams. Beginning and ending 1 cm (¼ in) inside the ms borders of the main part of the jacket, sew cast-off edge of collar neatly to the neck edge. Sew 2 small buttons on right border, and carefully part ms on left hand border to act as buttonholes.

Cecil's leggings

Beginning at the waist edge of the first leg, and using 3.00 mm (11) (US 2–3) needles and MC, cast on 36 sts.

Work 2 rows in k1, p1 rib.

Ribbon-hole row *(k1, p1) twice, m1, p2 tog, rep from * to end.

Work 5 rows in k1, p1 rib.

Work 2 rows in st st, then inc 1 st at both ends of next row and every following 4th row, until the 5th inc row has been worked (46 sts).

To shape leg

Cast off 5 sts at the beginning of the next 2 rows, then dec 1 st at the beginning only of every row until 30 st remain.

Work 3 rows straight, in st st, then dec 1 st at both ends of the next row and every following 4th row, until the 3rd dec row has been worked (24 sts).

Work 4 rows in k1, p1 rib.

Work 11 rows in st st beginning with a purl row.

Dec row k2 tog, all along row (12 sts).

Next row p3 tog all along row. Cast off.

Work another leg the same.

To make up

Join the front and back seams. Sew inside leg seams. Thread ribbon or elastic through slots at waist.

Cecil's beret

With 3.00 mm (11) (US 2–3) needles and MC, cast on 44 sts.
Work 4 rows in k1, p1 rib.
5th row   Inc in every st all along row (88 sts).
6th row   Purl.
7th row   Knit.
Rep the last 2 rows twice, then the 6th row again.
Join in C and work the pattern as follows:
1st row   *k2 C, k2 MC, rep from * to end of row.
2nd row   *p2 C, k2 MC, rep from * to end of row.
Rep the last two rows. Break off C.
1st row   *k6, k2 tog, rep from * to end of row.
2nd row and all alternate rows   Purl.
3rd row   *k5, k2 tog, rep from * to end of row.
5th row   *k4, k2 tog, rep from * to end of row.
7th row   *k3, k2 tog, rep from * to end of row
9th row   *k2, k2 tog, rep from * to end of row.
11th row   *k1, k2 tog, rep from * to end of row.
13th row   k1, *k2 tog, rep from * to end of row, break off
wool leaving a long end.

To make up
Pass thread double through a darning needle, then thread
this through remaining sts and draw up tight. Sew up seam.
If you wish, you may make a small pom-pom to go on top
of beret.

Cecil's jumper

Back
With 3.00 mm (11) (US 2–3) needles and MC, cast on 36 sts.
Work 6 rows in k1, p1 rib.
Work 2 rows in st st. Join in C.
1st row   *k2 C, k2 MC, rep from * to end of row.
2nd row   *p2 C, p2 MC, rep from * to end of row,
Rep the last 2 rows. Break off C.
Work 14 rows in st st.

To shape armholes
Cast off 4 sts at beginning of the next 2 rows (26 sts).
Work 10 rows in st st.

To shape neck
k9, cast off 8, knit to end.
On the last 9 sts   p7, p2 tog. Cast off.
Rejoin wool to neck edge and p2 tog, p7.

Front
Work exactly the same as the Back until armhole shaping
has been completed (26 sts).
Work 8 rows in st st.

To shape the neck
1st row   k9, cast off 8, knit to end.
Next row   Purl the last remain 9 sts.
Next row   k2 tog, knit to end of row.
Work 2 rows in st st beginning with a purl row. Cast off.
With wrong side of work facing rejoin in wool at neck edge,
and purl to the end of the row.
Next row   Knit until last 2 sts, k2 tog.
Work 2 rows in st st beginning with a purl row. Cast off.

Sleeves
With 3.00 mm (11) (US 2–3) needles and MC, cast on 18 sts.
Work 4 rows in k1, p1 rib.
Next row   Inc in each st along row (36 sts).
Next row   Purl
Work 8 rows in st st.

To shape sleeve top
Dec 1 st at each end of every row until 24 sts remain. Cast
off.
Work a second sleeve in the same way.

To make up
Join the shoulder seams for about 1 cm (¼ in) in from
armhole end. Sew sleeves into armholes.
Join sleeve and side seams. Work a row of dc (US sc) along
the front and back neck edges. Sew a small button on to each
back shoulder and make a buttonhole loop on each front
shoulder.

Cecil's short pants

Back
With 3.00 mm (11) (US 2–3) needles and C, cast on 36 sts.
Work 6 rows in k1, p1 rib.
Next 2 rows   k24, turn (this completes 1 row), sl1, p11.
Next 2 rows   sl1, k17, turn: sl1, p23, turn.
Next row   sl1, then knit to end of row.
Next row   Purl.
** Inc 1 st at both ends of next row and every following 4th
row until the 4th inc row has been worked (44sts).
Work 3 rows straight.

To shape leg openings
Cast off 3 sts at the beginning of the next 10 rows. Cast off.

Front
Work 6 rows of k1, p1 rib, then rep from ** on the Back to
the end.

Leg bands
Join up side seams, then pick up 32 sts evenly around one
leg edge.

Work 4 rows of k1, p1 rib. Cast off.
Work other leg band the same way.

To make up
Join the under leg seams, and thread thin elastic through ribbing at waist.

Cecilia's dress

Front
With 3.00 mm (11) (US 2–3) needles and MC, cast on 72 sts.
Work 4 rows in ms. Join in C.
1st row   *k2 C, k2 MC, rep from * to end.
2nd row   *p2 C, p2 MC, rep from * to end.
3rd row   As 1st row
4th row   As 2nd row. Break off C.
Using MC, work 28 rows in st st.
Next row   k2 tog all along the row (36 sts).***
Work 5 rows in st st beginning with a purl row.

Shape armholes
Cast off 6 sts at the beginning of the next 2 rows (24 sts).
Work 2 rows in st st.
Work the 4 pattern rows as given on the bottom of the dress, break off C.
Work 2 rows in st st.

To shape the neck
k 8, cast off 8 sts, knit to end of row.
On the last 8 sts work as follows:
Next row   Purl.
Next row   k2 tog, knit to end of row (7 sts).
Work 2 rows in st st. Cast off remaining 7 sts.
Rejoin wool to other side of neck and purl 1 row.
Next row   Knit 6 sts, k2 tog.
Work 2 rows in st st. Cast off remaining 7 sts.

Back
Work exactly the same as Front to*** (36 sts).

Left half back
Next row   p18, turn and cast on 4 sts for underlap (22 sts).
1st row   Knit.
2nd row   Purl to last 4 sts, k4.
Rep the last 2 rows once, then the first row again.

Shape the armhole
Cast off 6 sts, purl to last 4 sts, k4 (16 sts).
Work 12 rows in st st, knitting the 4 underlap sts in every row.

To shape neck
Cast off 8 sts, knit remaining sts.
Next row   Purl to last 2 sts, p2 tog. Cast off.

Right half back
Rejoin wool to the 18 remaining sts, and with the wrong side of the work facing, cast on 4 sts (22 sts).
1st row   k4, purl to end of the row.
2nd row   Knit.
Rep the last 2 rows once, and first row again.

Shape the armhole
Cast off 6 sts, then knit to end of row (16 sts).
Work 12 rows in st st, keeping the knit 4 in each row for the underlap.

To shape the neck
Cast off 8, purl to end of row.
Next row   Knit until last 2 sts, k2 tog. Cast off.

Sleeves
Begin at the arm edge with 3.00 mm (11) (US 2–3) needles and MC, cast on 18 sts.
Work 4 rows in ms.
Next row   Inc in every st all along row (36 sts).
Next row   Purl.
Work 8 rows in st st.

To shape sleeve top
Dec 1 st at both ends of every row until 24 sts remain. Cast off.
Work another sleeve the same.

To make up
Join the shoulder seams. Set the sleeves into the armholes, then sew up the sleeve and side seams. Sew the bottom of the underlap in position, with the left hand side under the right hand back. Sew 2 buttons on the left hand back 4 st border and make two buttonholes on the right hand back. Work 2 rows of dc (US sc) around the neck.

Cecilia's panties

Back
With 3.00 mm (11) (US 2–3) needles and MC, cast on 36 sts.
Work 4 rows in k1, p1 rib.
1st row   k24, turn.
2nd row   sl1, p11, turn.
3rd row   sl1, k17, turn.
4th row   sl1, p23, turn.
5th row   sl1, then knit to end of row.
6th row   Purl.
** Work 2 rows in st st, then inc 1 st at each end of the needle in the next row, and every following 4th row, until 40 sts are on needle.
Work 3 rows in st st starting with a purl row.

To shape leg openings
Dec 1 st at both ends of the needle in every row, until 16 sts remain. Cast off.**

Front
Cast on 36 sts and work 4 rows in ms, then work as for Back from ** to **.

To make up
Join the side seams and under leg seams. Work a round of dc (US sc) around the leg opening, then * 4ch, miss 1dc (US sc), sl st into next dc, rep from * all around leg. Fasten off. Work edging around the other leg. Thread thin elastic through waist.

Cecilia's jacket

Work as Cecil's jacket, but use the same colours as used in Cecilia's dress. When working the first part of the jacket, work only 4 rows of ms, then 2 rows of st st, 4 rows of pattern, and 8 rows of st st before the decrease for the waistline.
Work the Left front, Back, and Right front, same as for Cecil's jacket, but work only 4 rows of ms, 2 rows of st st, 4 rows of pattern, and 8 rows of st st before the decrease for the waistline. Sleeves and collar as per Cecil's jacket,

Cecilia's pixie hood

With 3.00 mm (11) (US 2–3) needles and MC, cast on 128 sts.
Work 3 rows in ms.
Next row Cast off 36 st, k55 (plus 1 st on needle = 56), cast off 36 sts (the cast off pieces act as ribbon ties for hood).
With right side of work facing rejoin wool to the centre 56 sts and work as follows:
1st row Knit.
2nd row k4, p until 4 sts remain, k4.
Rep the 1st and 2nd rows.
1st pattern row k4, join in C and work thus, *k2 C, k2 M, rep from * to 4 sts remain, k4 M.
2nd pattern row k4, *p2 C, p2 M, rep from * to 4 sts remain, k4 M.
Rep the last 2 rows.
Work 18 rows in st st keeping the k4 border at each end of row.

Shape the back of the hood
Cast off 8 sts at beginning of the next 2 rows.
Cast off 4 sts at the beginning only of every row until 16 sts remain. Cast off.

To make up
Fold the hood in half widthwise and join the cast off edges together neatly to form the back of hood.

Darryl and Meryl

Based on a 1950s pattern by Patons, the two outfits, one for a boy doll and one for a girl doll, are quickly knitted in 5-ply, and are suitable for 41 cm (16 in) dolls. By using different stripe combinations in the two jumpers (sweaters), the two outfits can look completely different, although the actual number of stitches, rows, etc. used are the same.

Materials

50 g (2 oz) 5-ply in MC for Darryl's pants and jumper
Small amount of 5-ply in C for Darryl's jumper
Small amount of 5-ply in W for Darryl's jumper
50 g (2 oz) 5-ply in MC for Meryl's skirt and jumper
50 g (2 oz) 5-ply in W or C for Meryl's jumper and panties
1 pair 3.25 mm (10) (US 3) knitting needles

Measurements

Darryl

Trousers

Waist to crutch	10 cm	(4 in)
Width around waist	22 cm	(8½ in)
Length of side seam	12.5 cm	(5 in)
Inside leg	4 cm	(1½ in)

Jumper

Shoulder to hem	13 cm	(5 in)
Width around chest	28 cm	(11 in)
Side seam	7 cm	(2¾ in)
Armhole	5.5 cm	(2¼ in)

Meryl

Jumper

Shoulder to hem	13 cm	(5 in)
Width around chest	28 cm	(11 in)
Side seam	7 cm	(2¾ in)
Armhole	5 cm	(2 in)

Skirt

Waist to hem	13.5 cm	(5¼ in)
Width around waist	28 cm	(11 in)
Width around hem (unstretched)	38 cm	(15 in)

Panties

Waist to crutch	11 cm	(4¼ in)
Width around waist	23 cm	(9 in)
Side seam (include leg ribbing)	8.5 cm	(3¼ in)

Tension

7 sts = 2.5 cm (1 in)

Darryl's trousers

Two pieces alike

With 3.25 mm (10) (US 3) needles and MC, cast on 32 sts (waist).
Work 4 rows in k1, p1 rib.
Work 26 rows in st st.
Work 6 rows in k1 p1 rib. Cast off in rib.
Make another piece the same.

To make up

Join the bottom of each leg together along the length of the bottom ribbing. Join up front and back seam. Thread hat elastic, or other thin elastic, through ribbing at waist.

Darryl's jumper

Back and Front alike

With 3.25 mm (10) (US 3) needles and MC, cast on 38 sts.
Work 6 rows in k1, p1 rib.
Proceed in strip as follows:
1st row   Knit in C.
2nd row   Purl in C.
3rd row   Knit in W.
4th row   Purl in W.
5th row   As per first row.
6th row   As per 2nd row.
7th row   Knit in MC.
8th row   Purl in MC.
Rep the last 8 rows 3 times, then rows 1–6 again.
Work 4 rows of st st using MC. Cast off loosely.
Join 8 sts of each shoulder starting from armhole end.

Sleeve bands

With right side facing you, pick up 36 sts, starting at end of 2nd stripe pattern, and working along one side, past the shoulder seam and down to corresponding point on other side.

Work 5 rows in k1, p1 rib. Cast off loosely in rib. Work other sleeve band to match.

To make up

Sew up side seams. Work 1 row of dc (US sc) around neck with MC.

Meryl's jumper

Back

**With 3.25 mm (10) (US 3) needles and MC, cast on 38 sts.

Work 6 rows of k1, p1 rib.

Stripe pattern

4 rows of st st in C.

2 rows of st st in MC.

Rep stripe pattern 4 times, then 4 rows of C once.**

Work 4 rows of MC.

Cast off.

Front

Work from ** to ** as given for Back.

Work 2 rows of sts in MC.

Next row   k12, cast off 14 sts, work to end of row.

Next row   p10, p2 tog. Cast off.

Rejoin wool to other side and, with wrong side of work facing, p2 tog, purl to end of row. Cast off.

To make up

Join up shoulder seams for 8 sts and work sleeve-bands as on Darryl's jumper.

Front neckband

Miss 2 sts from shoulder and pick up 24 sts around neck edge. Work 5 rows in k1, p1 rib. Cast off.

Back neckband

Miss 2 sts from shoulder and pick up 20 sts along back neck edge. Work 5 rows in k1, p1 rib. Cast off.

To make up

Join side seams. Fasten both sides of neck with a small snap fastener.

Meryl's skirt

Back and front alike

With 3.25 mm (10) (US 3) needles and MC, cast on 70 sts.

1st row   k1, *k5, p2, rep from * to last 6 sts, k6.

2nd row   k1, *p5, k2, rep from * to last 6 sts, p5, k1.

Rep the last 2 rows 19 times (40 rows).

Next row   k2, *k2 tog, rep from * to end.

Commencing with a purl row, work 9 rows in st st (for waistband).

To make up

Sew up side seams. Fold over waistband and carefully stitch down on wrong side of work, leaving opening for elastic. Thread elastic through waistband to size of doll's waist.

Meryl's panties

With 3.25 mm (10) (US 3) needles and W, cast on 31 sts.

1st row   *k1, p1, rep from * to last st, k1.

2nd row   k2, *p1, k1, rep from * to last st, k1.

3rd row   k1, *w fwd k2 tog, rep from * to end.

4th row   As 2nd row

5th row   As first row.

Work 18 rows in st st.

Shape leg openings

Dec 1 st at at both ends of every row until 7 sts remain.

Work 5 rows in st st. Cast off.

Work another piece exactly the same.

To make up

Join side seams. Pick up 38 sts around each leg opening and work 5 rows in k1, p1 rib. Cast off.

Join back and front pieces together, and thread elastic through holes at waist.

Ernest and Ernestine

Many doll collectors have tiny dolls, which are just crying out to be dressed. Dolls measuring approximately 15–18 cm (6–7 in) manufactured in bisque, celluloid or plastic, have been so popular over the last 50 years or more, that these patterns, originally published in the late 1940s, one for a girl doll and one for a boy doll, have been adapted so that they are ideal for many small dolls.

Materials
25 g (1 oz) 2-ply wool in MC (is enough for both outfits)
Small ball of 2-ply wool in C for Ernestine's outfit
Small ball of 2-ply wool in C for Ernest's outfit
1 pair of 2.25 mm (13) (US 1) knitting needles
Narrow white ribbon

Measurements

Ernest

Jacket
Shoulder to hem	7 cm	(2¾ in)
Around chest at armholes	17cm	(6¾ in)
Width of hem	26 cm	(10¾ in)
Sleeve seam	3cm	(1¾ in)

Leggings
Front waist to crutch	5 cm	(2 in)
Back waist to crutch	6 cm	(2⅜ in)
Around waist	15 cm	(6 in)
Inside leg to bottom of foot	6 cm	(2⅜ in)
Outside leg to toe	11 cm	(4¼ in)

Cap
Circumference	15 cm	(6 in)
Rim to crown	5.5cm	(2¼ in)
Edge turnback brim to crown	4 cm	(1½ in)

Ernestine

Dress
Shoulder to hem	9.5 cm	(3¾ in)
Width around hem	23 cm	(9 in)
Width around chest	17 cm	(6¾ in)
Sleeve seam	1.25 cm	(½ in)

Jacket
Shoulder to hem	6 cm	(2⅜ in)
Width around hem	23.5cm	(9¼ in)
Width around chest	18 cm	(7 in)
Length of sleeve seam	2.5cm	(1 in)

Panties
Waist to crutch	5 cm	(2 in)
Width around waist	12.5 cm	(5 in)
Side seam	3.5 cm	(1½ in)

Bonnet
Brim to crown	5cm	(2 in)
Width around face	10cm	(4 in)

Tension
9 sts = 2.5 cm (1 in)

Ernestine's dress

Front
Note Sleeves are worked as part of front and back pieces.
With 2.25 mm (13) (US1) needles and C, cast on 51 sts.
Work 4 rows in garter st. Break off wool
Join in MC and work lacy pattern as follows:
1st row   *(k1, m1, k3, sl1, k2 tog, psso, k3, m1), rep from * to 1 st remains, k1.
2nd row   Purl.
3rd row   As per first row.
4th row   Purl.
5th row   As per first row.
6th row   Knit.
Rep these 6 rows three times.
Dec row *k2 tog, k2 tog, k1, rep from * to last st, k1 (31 sts).
Ribbon row   p1, *(wrn, p2 tog), rep from * to end.
Work 4 rows in st st.

Sleeve
Cast on 4 sts at beginning of next 2 rows.
Work 6 rows in st st.

PATTERN ON PAGE 24

With her fancy patterned 2-ply knitted jacket draped over an old miniature ormolu chair, Ernestine, a 18 cm (7 in) bisque headed S.F.B.J./60/Paris baby doll, plays happily with her little brown celluloid doll. Sitting beside her, in his complementing outfit is Ernest, a bisque headed Made in Germany/206.2 3/o baby doll, trying to decide whether to play with his miniature rocking horse or his train set.

PATTERN ON PAGE 28

'What story do we pick to read today?' asks Freda, a 43 cm (17 in) Chad Valley English cloth doll, of Frederick, a 43 cm (17 in) oiled cloth mask face doll by Dean's of England. Dressed in their 1930s style 4-ply outfits with matching berets, they are ready for anything.

PATTERN ON PAGE 31

'How does your toy work?' ask Gabrielle, a 33 cm (13 in) bisque headed German Armand Marseille Dream Baby, A.M./ 351 2½ K, as she securely holds onto her old Victorian rattle. 'Mine has a whistle in the handle.' Gabriel, a German Baehr and Proeschild 532, bisque headed, fully jointed, open/closed mouth doll dressed in rompers, with matching double moss stitch motif, plays unperturbed with his key-wind papier-mâché egg with trembling birds.

PATTERN ON PAGE 34

'Give poor old Teddy a friendly pat,' says Henry, a 36 cm (14 in) sprayed bisque D.P.C. England doll on a cloth body, to cousin Henrietta, a 34 cm (13½ in) PPM/K Polish celluloid. Dressed in matching 3-ply outfits with Fair Isle jumpers, they are dressed ready for play, even if the weather is a little chilly outside.

Next row   k14, cast off 11 sts, knit to end of row.
Work 4 rows of st st on these last 14 sts. Cast off.
Join wool to neck end of remaining sts, and work 4 rows.
Cast off.

Back
Work as for front, until ribbon row has been worked.
Next row   k14, turn and work 3 rows of st st on these 14 sts.

Sleeve
**Cast on 4 sts at start of next row, then work 8 more rows
of st st.
Next row   Cast off 5 sts for neck.
Work 3 rows in st st. Cast off.*
Rejoin wool to end of sts on needle, and k2 tog, then knit to
end of row.
Work 4 rows, then work other side of Back as from ** to *.

To make up
Join shoulder, sleeve and underarm seams. Using C, work
crochet edging around neck and end of each sleeve.
Work a row of dc (US sc) around edges of back opening and
fasten with small beads or buttons. Thread ribbon through
ribbon holes at waist, sleeves and neck, (if needed) and tie
ribbons in a bow to finish off.

Ernestine's jacket

Back
With 2.25 mm (13) (US 1) needles and C, cast on 41 sts.
Work 4 rows in garter st.
Change to MC, and then work the 6 lacy pattern rows as
given for the Dress, twice.
Dec row   *k2, k2 tog, rep from * till 1 st remains, k1.
Next row   p31.

Armhole
Continuing working in st st, cast off 2 sts at the beginning of
the next 2 rows.
Work 12 rows in st st.
Cast off 9 sts at beginning of next 2 rows (for shoulders).
Cast off remaining sts (neck).

Right front
With 2.25 mm (13) (US 1) needles and C, cast on 25 sts.
Work 4 rows garter st. Break off C.
With MC:
1st pattern row   k4 (border), *k1, m1, k3, sl1, k2 tog, psso,
k3, m1, rep from * to last st, k1.
2nd row   Purl to last 4 sts, k4.
3rd row   As first row.
4th row   As 2nd row.
5th row   As first row.

6th row   Knit.
Rep the last 6 rows once.
Next row   k5, *k2 tog, k2, rep from * to end (20 sts).
Continuing with garter st border work 2 rows in st st.

***Armhole*
Cast off 2 sts at beginning of next row, and dec 1 st at
armhole edge on next row.
Work 11 rows in st st, keeping the 4 garter st border.
Next row   Cast off 8 sts at beginning of row for neck.
Work 2 rows in st st. Cast off.**

Left front
With 2.25 (13) (US 1) needles and C, cast on 25 sts.
Work 4 rows in garter st. Break off C.
Using MC:
1st row   k1, *m1, k3, sl1, k2 tog, psso, k3, m1, k1 rep from
* to last 4 sts, k4.
2nd row   k4, purl to end.
3rd row   As first row.
4th row   As 2nd row.
5th row   As first row.
6th row   Knit.
Rep the last 6 rows once.
Next row   *k2, k2 tog, rep to last 5 sts, k5.
Next row   k4, purl to end.
Work as per Right Front from ** to **.

Sleeves
With 2.25cm (13) (US 1) needles and C, cast on 21 sts.
Work 3 rows in garter st. Break off C.
Join in MC and work the 6 rows of fancy pattern as given
for dress.
Work 6 rows in st st (can be more or less rows according to
length of sleeve).

Shape top
Cast off 2 sts at start of next 2 rows, and then dec 1 st at each
end of next row.
Work 3 rows in st st. Cast off.

Collar
With 2.25 mm (13) (US 1) needles and C, cast on 33 sts.
Knit 6 rows in garter st. Cast off loosely.

To make up
Sew up shoulder seams. Sew sleeves in position in
armholes, then sew up sleeve and side seams. Place collar in
position, 3 sts in from each of the front edges, sew in place.
Close with snap fasteners and then decorate front with tiny
buttons.

Ernestine's panties

With 2.25 mm (13) (US 1) needles and MC, cast on 28 sts.
Work 4 rows in k1, p1 rib.
Work 12 rows in st st.
Cast off 2 sts at beginning of next 10 rows.
Work 6 rows straight in st st, then cast on 2 sts at beginning of next 10 rows.
Work 12 rows in st st without further shaping.
Work 4 rows in k1, p1 rib. Cast off in rib.
Work tiny crochet chain loop edging around each leg.

To make up
Join up side seams. If necessary, thread thin hat elastic through ribbing at waist to suit doll.

Ernestine's bonnet

With 2.25 mm (13) (US 1) needles and C, cast on 41 sts.
Work 4 rows in garter st. Break off C.
Join in MC and work 6 lacy pattern rows (as given for front of dress) twice, dec 1 st at end of last row.
1st row   *k6, k2 tog, rep from * to end of row.
2nd and every alternate row   Purl.
3rd row   *k5, k2 tog, rep from * to end of row.
5th row   *k4, k2 tog, rep from * to end of row.
7th row   *k3, k2 tog, rep from * to end of row.
9th row   *k2, k2 tog, rep from * to end of row.
Break off wool. Using a darning needle, run end through remaining sts, draw up and fasten off securely.

To make up
Join seam from crown to beginning of st st rows. Sew ribbons at front edges to tie.

Ernest's jacket

Back
With 2.25 mm (13) (US 1) needles and C, cast on 41 sts and work 4 rows in garter st. Break off C.
Join in MC and work 12 rows in st st.
Dec row   *k2, k2 tog, rep from * to last st, k1.
Purl 1 row.
Knit 2 rows in C. Break off C.
Using MC work 2 rows in st st.
Cast off 3 sts at beginning of next 2 rows.
Work 12 rows in st st.
Cast off 9 sts at beginning of next 2 rows (shoulder).
Cast off remaining sts.

Left front
With 2.25 mm (13) (US 1) needles and C, cast on 25 sts and work 4 rows in garter st. Break off C.
Join in MC and work as follows:
Next row   Knit.
Next row   k4, purl to end.
Rep last 2 rows 5 times.
Next row   *k2 tog, k2, rep from * to 5 sts from end, k5.
Next row   k4, purl to end.
Keeping the 4 st garter stitch border, proceed as follows:
With C, work 2 rows in garter st. Break off C.
Work 2 rows of st st.

Armholes
**Cast off 2 sts at beginning of next row, and dec 1 st, at armhole edge on next row.
Work 11 rows in st st.
Cast off 8 sts for neck at beginning of next row.
Work 2 rows. ** Cast off.

Right front
With 2.25 mm (13) (US 1) needles and C, cast on 25 sts.
Knit 4 rows in garter st. Break off C.
Join in MC and work as follows:
Next row   Knit
Next row   Purl to last 4 sts, k4.
Rep last 2 rows 5 times.
Next row   k5, *k2 tog, k2, rep from * to end.
Next row   Purl to last 4 sts, k4.
Keeping the 4 st garter stitch border, proceed as follows:
With C, work 2 rows in garter st. Break off C.
Work 1 row in st st, starting with a purl row.

Armholes to finish
Work from ** to ** as given for Left front. Cast off.

Sleeves
With 2.25 mm (13) (US 1) needles and C, cast on 21 sts.
Work 3 rows. Break off C.
Join in MC and work 12 rows of st st.

To shape sleeve top
Cast off 2 sts at beginning of next 2 rows, then dec 1 st at each end of next row.
Work 3 rows in st st. Cast off.
Make another sleeve the same.

Collar
With 2.25 mm (13) (US 1) needles and C, cast on 33 sts.
Work 6 rows in garter st. Cast off loosely.

To make up
Sew sleeves into armholes, then sew up sleeve and side seams. Pin collar in place, 3 sts from each of the front edges. Sew in place. Sew two tiny snap fasteners in place on front edges, then sew buttons on left front as decoration.

Ernest's leggings

Right leg
**With 2.25 mm (13) (US 1) needles and MC, begin at the waist edge by casting on 28 sts.
Work 2 rows in k1, p1 rib.
Ribbon row   *k1, m1, k2 tog, p1, rep from * to end of row.
Work 2 rows in k1, p1 rib.**
Purl 1 row.

To shape back (working in st st)
Next 2 rows   k6, turn for first row, sl1, purl back for 2nd row.
Next 2 rows   k12, turn, sl1, purl back.
Next 2 rows   k18, turn, sl1, purl back.
Next 2 rows   Work across all sts.
***Inc 1 st at both ends of needle in the next and following 6th row (32 sts).
Work 5 rows in st st.

To shape leg
Dec 1 st at the beginning of the next 16 rows (16 sts).
Work 4 rows in st st.
Ribbon row   *k1, m1, k2 tog, rep from * until 1 st remains, k1.
Purl one row.

Instep and foot
Next row   k11, turn, p6, turn, leaving 5 sts unworked at each end.
Work 5 rows of st st on the centre 6 sts (instep).
Next row   With the working needle, pick up and k4 sts from the row ends at side of instep, then knit the 5 sts left unworked.
Next row   k15, pick up and k4 sts from the row ends at opposite side of instep, k5 (24 sts).
Work 2 rows in garter st.

Shape heel and toe
1st row   k1, k2 tog, k5, k2 tog, k4, k2 tog, k5, k2 tog, k1.
2nd row   Knit.
3rd row   k1, k2 tog, k4, k2 tog, k2, k2 tog, k4, k2 tog, k1 (16 sts). Cast off.***

Left leg
Work the ribbing from ** to ** as given for right leg.

Shape the back
Knit one row.
Next 2 rows   p6, turn, sl1, k5.
Next 2 rows   p12, turn, sl1, k11.
Next 2 row   p18, turn, sl1, k17.
Work 3 rows in st st.
Work rest of leg as per right leg from *** to ***.

To make up
Sew up the centre front and centre back seams, then sew the leg and underfoot seams. Thread fine ribbon through waist holes and through holes at ankles, then tie each ribbon in a bow.

Ernest's hat

With 2.25 mm (13) (US 1) needles and C, cast on 54 sts.
Work 4 rows of garter sts. Break off C.
Join in MC, work 4 rows of k1, p1 rib.
Work 10 rows st st.
1st row   *k7, k2 tog, rep from * to end.
2nd and all alternate rows   Purl.
3rd row   *k6, k2 tog, rep from * to end.
5th row   *k5, k2tog, rep from * to end.
7th row   *k4, k2 tog, rep from * to end.
9th row   *k3, k2 tog, rep from * to end.
11th row   *k2, k2 tog, rep from * to end.
Break off wool, run end through remaining sts, draw up and fasten off securely.
Sew seam from top of crown to brim. Turn brim back to k1, p1 rib.

Freda and Frederick

These outfits are based on an original set of boy and girl doll's clothes patterns, which were first published in the 1930s. They were to be worn by 41–43 cm (16–17 in) composition and bisque headed dolls of that era. Although the outfits are very '30s' in appearance, they can look equally at home on all types of dolls, no matter their age.

Materials

50 g (2 oz) 4-ply wool for Freda's jumper and beret
50 g (2 oz) 4-ply wool for Freda's skirt
25 g (1 oz) 2-ply wool in white for Freda's panties
50 g (2 oz) 4-ply wool for Frederick's jumper and beret
25 g (1 oz) 4-ply wool for Frederick's pants
1 pair of 3.00 mm (11) (US 2–3) knitting needles

Measurements

Freda

Jumper
Shoulder to hem	16 cm	(6¼ in)
Width around chest	28 cm	(11 in)
Sleeve seam	9.5 cm	(3¾ in)

Skirt
Waist to hem	14 cm	(5½ in)
Width around waist	20 cm	(8 in)
Width around hem (unstretched)	28 cm	(11 in)

Beret
Circumference	24 cm	(9½ in)
Brim to crown	9 cm	(3½ in)

Panties
Waist to crutch	12 cm	(4¾in)
Width around waist	26.5 cm	(10½ in)
Side seam	7.5 cm	(3 in)

Frederick

Jumper
Shoulder to hem	16 cm	(6¼ in)
Width around chest	28 cm	(11 in)
Sleeve seam	9 cm	(3½ in)

Trousers
Front waist to crutch	10 cm	(4 in)
Back waist to crutch	12 cm	(4¾ in)
Width around waist	27 cm	(10½ in)
Side seam	14 cm	(5½in)
Inside leg seam	1.5 cm	(½ in)

Beret
Circumference	22 cm	(8½ in)
Brim to crown	9 cm	(3½ in)

Tension
8 sts = 2.5 cm (1 in)

Freda's jumper

Back
With 3.00 mm (11) (US 2–3) needles, cast on 40 sts.
Work 8 rows in k1, p1 rib.
Work in pattern as follows:
1st row   * p1, k3, rep from * to end of row.
2nd row   p2, *k1, p3, rep from * to last 2 sts, k1, p1.
3rd row   k2, *p1, k3, rep from * to last 2 sts, p1, k1.
4th row   Purl.
Rep these last 4 rows 6 times.

Armholes
Continuing in pattern, k2 tog at beg of every row until 32 sts remain.**
Work 16 rows (4 patterns).
Next row   Work 10 sts, cast off 12 sts, k10.
Keeping continuity of pattern, work 5 rows on the last 10 st.
Cast off.
Join in wool to other side and work 5 rows. Cast off.

Front
Work as per Back to **.
Work 4 rows in pattern.

Neck opening
Work 16 sts in pattern and turn.
Work 12 rows in pattern.
Cast off 6 sts at neck edge and then work rows 2–4 of pattern, then rows 1–3 of pattern. Cast off.
Rejoin wool at neck opening and work 12 rows in pattern.
Work neck from *** to ***.

Sleeves
With 3.00 mm (11) (US 2–3) needles, cast on 28 sts and work 6 rows of k1, p1 rib.
Working the 4 pattern rows as given for back of jumper, inc 1 st at each end of every 4th row, until there are 40 sts on the needle. Work 1 pattern.
Cast off 2 sts at beg of every row until 20 sts remain. Cast off.
Work another sleeve the same.

Collar
With 3.00 mm (11) (US 2–3) needles, cast on 60 sts.
Work 3 rows in garter st.
Work the 4 rows of pattern as given for back of jumper.
1st row   *k8, k2 tog, rep from * to end of row.
2nd row   Purl.
3rd row   *k7, k2 tog, rep from * to end of row.
4th row   Purl. Cast off.

To make up
Sew up shoulder seams and sew sleeves in position. Sew up sleeve and side seams. Sew collar in place.
If you wish to give the jumper the 30s look, make a chain in crochet and lace through neck opening. Finishing each end with a tiny pom-pom. These are made by winding wool around the finger, fasten off at one end, cut and trim, then sew onto each end of chain.
   Otherwise work a row of dc (US sc) down each side of opening, then on one side, make a row of tiny loops in chain st. Sew buttons on the other side to match loops, or just make a loop at neck edge and sew on a button to match.

Freda's skirt

With 3.00 mm (11) (US 2–3) needles, cast on 145 sts.
Knit 1 row.
Next row   k3, p2.
Rep the last row 41 times. (This completes the skirt.)
Next row   *k2 tog, rep from * to last st, k1.
Work 8 rows in k1, p1 rib.

To make up
Sew up back seam. Fold over ribbing and sew. Thread elastic through to fit doll's waist.

Freda's beret

With 3.00 mm (11) (2–3) needles, cast on 80 sts.
Work 4 rows in k1, p1 rib.
Knit 1 row, knitting twice into every 8th st to last st, inc (90 sts).
Beginning with the 2nd row of pattern as given for jumper, work 4 complete patterns.
Working in st st proceed as follows.
1st row   *k7, k2 tog, rep from * to end of row.
2nd and every alternate row   Purl.
3rd row   *k6, k2 tog, rep from * to end of row.
5th row   *k5, k2 tog, rep from * to end of row.
7th row   *k4, k2 tog, rep from * to end of row.
9th row   *k3, k2 tog, rep from * to end of row.
11th row   *k2, k2 tog, rep from * to end of row.
13th row   *k1, k2 tog, rep from * to end of row.
Break off wool, thread the tail piece through remaining sts, draw up tight, and secure.

To make up
Sew up seam and, if you wish, make a pom-pom for the top of the beret.

Freda's panties

With 3.00 mm (11) (US 2–3) needles, cast on 54 sts.
Work 3 rows in k1, p1 rib.
Next row   k2 *m1, k2 tog, rep from * to end.
Work 5 rows in k1, p1 rib.
Work in the following ribbing pattern.
1st row   *k1, p1, rep from * to end of row
2nd row   Knit.
Rep the last 2 rows 14 times
Dec 1 st at beginning and end of every row until 26 sts remain.
Work 4 rows without decreasing.
Inc 1 st at each end of every row until there are 54 sts.
Continue in fancy 2-row rib pattern for 30 rows.
Work 8 rows in k1, p1 rib. Cast off.

To make up
Sew up side seams, and thread a length of elastic through holes at waist.
Work 3 rows of dc (US sc) around each leg opening.

Frederick's jumper

Work main part of front and back jumper to finish of armhole decreases as per Freda's jumper ** (36 sts).

Back
Work 16 rows in pattern.
Next row   Work 12 sts, cast off 12 sts, work 12 sts.
Work 3 rows on these last 12 sts. Cast off.
Join in wool to neck edge of other side and work 3 rows. Cast off.

Front
Work 12 rows in pattern.
Next row   Work 12 st, cast off 12 sts, work 12 sts.
Work 7 rows on the last 12 sts. Cast off.
Join in wool to neck edge of other side and work 7 rows. Cast off.

To make up
Join up right hand shoulder seam, then pick up 76 sts around neck. Work 22 rows in k1, p1 rib. Cast off loosely.
Sew up 1 cm (1/4 in) of left shoulder seam from armhole edge. Sew sleeves into position. Sew up sleeve and side seams. Work 2 small loops on the front edge of left shoulder and along ribbing. Sew buttons to match on the back of shoulder and ribbing.

Frederick's knickers

With 3.00 mm (11) (US 2–3) needles, cast on 48 sts and work 4 rows of k1, p1 rib.
Working st st:
1st row   Work 4 sts, turn and work back.
3rd row   Work 8 sts, turn and work back.
5th row   Work 12 sts, turn and work back.
7th row   Work 16 sts, turn and work back.
Continue in this way, working 4 more sts each time, until all stitches are on one needle.
Work 32 rows in st st (being sure to mark each end of 4th row with a coloured thread).

Shape back
1st row   Work 6 sts, turn and work back.
3rd row   Work 12 sts, turn and work back.
5th row   Work 18 sts, turn and work back.
Continue in this way, but working 12 sts each time, until all stitches are on one needle.
Work 4 rows in k1, p1 rib. Cast off.
Work another leg, but work 1 knit row, then proceed from * to end.

Gusset
Cast on 2 sts and working in st st:
Inc 1 st each end of every knit row until there are 12 sts.
Dec 1 st at each end of every knit row until 2 sts remain. Cast off.

To make up
Sew up seams. Sew gusset in place using coloured threads as markers. If needed, run a length of thin elastic through ribbing.

Frederick's beret

Work same as Freda's, but leave off pom-pom.

Gabrielle and Gabriel

These two lovely outfits are suitable for 30–33 cm (12–13 in) dolls: a romper suit for the boy doll in your life, accompanied by a matching dress and panties for your favourite girl doll. Although both outfits were originally designed independently in the early 1950s, I have adapted them to complement each other, and both outfits are suitable for dolls of all ages and types.

Materials
50 g (2 oz) 3-ply wool for Gabrielle's dress
25 g (1 oz) 2-ply wool in white for Gabrielle's panties
50 g (2oz) 3-ply wool for Gabriel's rompers
1 pair 3.00 mm (11) (US 2–3) knitting needles
1 pair 2.75mm (12) (2) knitting needles
2 snap fasteners or buttons for Gabrielle's dress
3 buttons for Gabriel's Romper suit

Measurements

Gabrielle

Dress
Shoulder to hem	16 cm	(6¼ in)
Width around chest	20 cm	(8 in)
Width around hem	62 cm	(24½ in)
Sleeve seam	2 cm	(¾ in)

Panties
Waist to crutch	8 cm	(3¼ in)
Width around waist	19 cm	(7½ in)
Side seam	5 cm	(2 in)

Gabriel

Rompers
Shoulder to bottom of leg	16 cm	(6¼ in)
Shoulder to waist	7 cm	(2¾ in)
Width around chest	18 cm	(7 in)
Sleeve seam	3 cm	(1¼ in)
Inside leg seam	2 cm	(¾ in)

Tension
Dress and rompers 8 sts = 2.5 cm (1 in)
Panties 9 sts = 2.5 cm (1 in)

Gabrielle's dress

Back
With 3.00 mm (11) (US 2–3) needles, cast on 100 sts.
1st row   *k2, p2, rep from * to end of row.
2nd row   *k2, p2, rep from * to end of row.
3rd row   *p2, k2, rep from * to end of row.
4th row   *p2, k2, rep from * to end of row.
These 4 rows constitute the 'double moss st pattern'.
Rep the last 4 rows once.
Work 28 rows in st st.

Right half back
Dec row   *k3 tog, rep from * 16 times, k2 turn, cast on 1 st.
1st row   k4, p15.
2nd row   Knit.
3rd row   As first row.
Keeping the garter st border, work the 4 rows of double moss st twice.
Still keeping the garter st border, work in double ms for the next two rows, while at the same time casting off 3 sts at the beg of the next row. Then dec 1 st at armhole end of the next row.
Working in st st and keeping the garter st border, dec 1 st at the armhole end of the next 2 rows (13 sts).
Work 7 rows in st st with the garter st border.

Shaping the neck
Next row   Cast off 7 sts, work to end.
Work 3 rows in st st. Cast off.

Left half back
With right side of work facing, rejoin wool to the remaining sts.
Cast on 3 sts, then k1, *k3 tog, rep from * to end of row.
Next row   p15, k4.
Next row   Knit.
3rd row   p15, k4.

Keeping the garter st border, work the 4 rows of double ms, twice.

Still keeping the garter st border, work 1 row of double ms.

Next row   Cast off 3 sts, work in double ms to last 4 st, k4.
Continue in st st, dec 1 st at armhole end of the next 3 rows (13 sts).

Work 7 rows in st st with the garter st border.

Shaping the neck
Next row   Cast off 7 sts, work to end.
Work 3 rows in st st. Cast off.

Front
With 3.00 mm (11) (US 2–3) needles, cast on 100 sts.
Work the 4 rows of double ms, twice.
Work 28 rows of st st.
Dec row   *k3 tog, rep from * to 1 st remains, k1 (34 sts).
Work 3 rows in st st.
Work the 4 rows of double ms, twice.

Armhole
Working in double ms cast off 3 sts at the beg of the next 2 rows.
Continuing in st st, dec 1 st at both ends of the next 3 rows (22 sts).
Work 5 rows in st st.

Divide for the neck and shoulders
Next row   k6, cast off 10 sts, knit to end.
On the last 6 sts work 3 rows in st st. Cast off.
Rejoin wool to wrong side of the remaining 6 sts, work 3 rows in st st. Cast off.

Sleeves
Using 3.00 mm (11) (US 2–3) needles, cast on 28 sts and work 2 rows in k1, p1 rib.
Inc row   *k1, inc, rep from * to last st, k1 (54 sts).
2nd row   Purl.
3rd row   Knit.
4th row   Purl.

To shape the sleeve top
Cast off 3 sts at the beg of the next 2 rows.
3rd row   k3 tog, at both ends of row.
4th row   p3 tog, at both ends of row (40 sts).
5th row   k19, k2 tog, knit to end.
6th row   p17, p2 tog, p1, p2 tog, purl to end.
7th row   k1, *k4 tog, rep from * to end of row (10 sts).
8th row   Purl. Cast off.
Work another sleeve to match.

Collar (two pieces alike)
With 3.00 mm (11) (US 2–3) needles, cast on 26 sts.
Work the first 2 rows of double ms.

Next row   Work 4 sts in double ms, knit to last 4 sts, work 4 st in double ms.
Next row   Work 4 sts in double ms, purl to last 4 sts, work 4 st in double ms.
Rep the last two rows once. Cast off.

To make up
Sew up shoulder seams, sew sleeves into armholes, then sew up sleeve and side seams. Place overlap at back in place and sew down carefully. Place the two collar pieces into position, meeting at centre front, but 2 sts in from back edges. Sew in place. Close back with snap fasteners. If you wish, place 2 tiny buttons on outer half of back.

Gabrielle's panties
Worked in one piece.
Beginning at the waist edge, with 2.75 mm (12) (US 2) needles and W, cast on 36 sts.
Work 4 rows in k1, p1 rib.
Working in st st, inc 1 st at both ends of the next row and following 4th rows, 3 times (44 sts).
Work 3 rows in st st.

Shaping the leg openings
Continuing in st st, cast off 3 sts at beg of the next 10 rows, then dec 1 st at both ends of the following 2 rows (10 sts).
Work 10 rows in st st.
Inc 1 st at both ends of the next 2 rows, then cast on 3 sts at the beg of the following 10 rows (44 sts).
Work 3 rows in st st, then dec 1 st at both ends of the next row and every following 4th row, 3 times (36 sts).
Work 4 rows in k1, p1 rib. Cast off in rib.

To make up
Sew up the side seams. Run narrow hat or shirring elastic through waist band to fit doll.

Gabriel's romper suit

Back
Using 2.75 mm (12) (US 2) needles, cast on 24 sts and work 4 rows in k1, p1 rib.
Knit 1 row, purl 1 row. Break off wool.
Work another piece the same.
Change to 3.00 mm (11) (US 2–3) needles.
** *1st row*   Knit twice into each of the first 17 sts, k7, cast on 12 sts, k7 of the next set of sts, k twice into each of the next 17 sts (94 sts).
2nd row   Purl.
3rd row   k41, rib 12, k41.
4th row   p41, rib 12, p41.

PATTERN ON PAGE 37

'Do you think the horse will jump through the hoops?' asks Iris of Ira, as they watch a trio of old Tinker Toy metal flats. Ira and Iris, dressed in their complementing 3-ply pram outfits, are twin 18 cm (7 in) Japanese celluloid baby dolls by Royal.

PATTERN ON PAGE 40

'Have you packed everything you need?' asks Julia, a 36 cm (14 in) hard plastic teen bodied doll by Palitoy, England, as she checks on her brother Julian, a 34 cm (13½ in) hard plastic English Roddy walking doll. Dressed in their matching 3-ply check patterned jumpers, they are ready for their first day at their new school.

PATTERN ON PAGE 42

'Look what I've just done!' says Kim, a 38 cm (15 in) German celluloid boy doll by Bruno Schmidt, marked Schultz Marke/a heart/ 36/40/Germany, as he shows off his building blocks to his sister Kimberley, a pretty 41 cm (16 in) Dutch celluloid doll with a stork trademark. Dressed in their lovely 3-ply 1930s style, simple-to-knit outfits, with decorative pattern motifs, the pair are ready for many hours of play.

PATTERN ON PAGE 45

'It's done like this,' explains Leslie, a 43 cm (17 in) hard plastic English Rosebud doll, as he shows his sister Lesley, a 43 cm (17 in) English vinyl twisting waist 'Baby First Love' by Pedigree, just how to hold the wooden hoop. Dressed in matching 5-ply outfits with a simple 2-stitch twist stitch, they are ready to try their hand at a game of Hoopla.

Shaping the gusset

5th row   k41,(k2 tog, k8, k2 tog), k41.

6th row   Purl.

7th row   k41, (k2 tog, k6, k2 tog), k41.

8th row   Purl.

Continue working in st st, dec in gusset area (in brackets) until only 2 sts remain.

Next row   p40, p2 tog, p2 tog, p40 (82 sts).

Continue in st st, dec 1 st at each end of next and every following 3rd row, until 74 sts remain.

Work 4 rows in st st.

Change to 2.75 mm (12) (US 2) needles.

Next row   k2 tog, (k3 tog, 10 times), k10, (k3 tog, 10 times), k2 tog (32 sts).

Work 5 rows in k1, p1 rib.

Change to 3.00 mm (11) (US 2–3) needles.

1st row   k18, leave remaining 14 st on spare needle or knitting pin.

2nd row   k4, p14.

3rd row   Knit to last 3 st, m1, k2 tog, k1.

4th row   k4, p14.

5th row   Knit.

6th row   k4, p14.

7th row   Cast off 2 sts, work in double ms (as per border on Gabriella's dress) to last 4 sts, knit.

8th row   k4, work in double ms to end.

9th row   Cast off 2 sts, work in double ms to last 4 sts, knit.

Continue without shaping, work 3 more rows in double ms keeping the 4 garter st border, and making a buttonhole on the 10th row after the first buttonhole.

Work 5 rows in st st, ending at neck edge.

Next row   Cast off 9 sts, purl to end.

Shape shoulder

Cast off 2 sts at armhole edge on next row, then work 1 more row in st st. Cast off.

Rejoin wool to remain sts, cast on 4 sts for underlap, and work 4 garter st border, armhole dec etc. to match other side.

Front

With 2.75 mm (12) (US 2) needles, cast on 24 sts and work 2 rows in k1, p1 rib.

Next row   Rib 2, m1, k2 tog, work in rib to end.

Next row   Work in rib pattern. Break off wool.

Work another piece the same, only making the buttonhole (m1, k2 tog) at opposite end of work.

Change to 3.00 mm (11) (US 2–3) needles and work as Back ** to ** at end of waist ribbing.

Front bodice

Change to 3.00 mm (11) (US 2–3) needles.

Work 6 rows in st st.

Cast off 2 sts at beg of next 2 rows.

Dec 1 st at each end of next row.

Purl 1 row.

1st row   *k2, p2, rep from * to last 2 sts, k2.

2nd row   *p2, k2, rep from * to last 2 sts, p2.

3rd row   *p2, k2, rep from * to last 2 sts, p2

4th row   *k2, p2, rep from * to last 2 sts, k2.

5th and 6th rows   Same as first and 2nd rows.

Shape neck

k10, cast off 6 sts, k10.

Continuing on the last set of 10 sts, purl 10.

Cast off 2 sts at beg of next 2 knit rows (neck edge).

Shape shoulder as for Back.

Rejoin wool to remaining 10 sts, and work other side to match.

Sleeves

Cast on 22 sts with 2.75 mm (12) (US 2) needles.

Work 2 rows in k1, p1 rib.

Change to 3.00 mm (11) (US 2–3) needles.

Next row   k4, inc in each of the next 14 sts, k4 (36sts).

Work 7 rows in st st.

Cast off 3 sts at beg of next 2 rows.

k2 tog at each end of the next, and each alternate, knit row.

Next row   *k2 tog, rep from * to end of row. Cast off.

To make up

Sew up shoulder seams. With 2.75 mm (12) (US 2) needles, pick up and knit 38 sts around neck.

Work 1 row in k1, p1 rib.

Next row   Rib to within 3 sts from end, m1 k2 tog, p1.

Work 2 rows in k1, p1 rib. Cast off loosely in rib.

Sew sleeves into position, and sew up sleeve and side seams. Sew buttons to match buttonholes on back gusset, and close remaining gusset with 2 small snap fasteners.

Henry and Henrietta

Although the knitting components for these two outfits originated over a period of more than 10 years, from the early 1950s through to the 1960s, they are ageless, and therefore suitable for many of the 36 cm (14 in) dolls of years past, as well as today's more modern plastic dolls. The girl doll's, set comprises a Fair-Isle jumper, plain skirt and panties. The boy doll's outfit is a Fair-Isle (front only) jumper, and plain matching trousers (or slacks).

Materials

50 g (2 oz) 3-ply in MC for Henry's jumper and trousers
50 g (2 oz) 3-ply in MC for Henrietta's jumper and skirt.
50 g (2 oz) 3-ply in W (this amount will also make both jumpers and Henrietta's pants)
1 pair 3.25 mm (10) (US 3) knitting needles
1 pair 3.00 mm (11) (US 2–3) knitting needles
1 pr 2.75 mm (12) (US 2) knitting needles
2 buttons for each jumper

Measurements

Henry

Jumper

Shoulder to hem	13 cm	(5 in)
Width around chest	24 cm	(9½ in)
Sleeve seam	9 cm	(3½ in)

Trousers (slacks)

Front waist to crutch	8 cm	(3¼ in)
Back waist to crutch	10 cm	(4 in)
Width around waist	20 cm	(8 in)
Outside leg seam	19.5 cm	(7¾ in)
Inside leg seam	12 cm	(4¾ in)

Henrietta

Jumper

Shoulder to hem	13 cm	(5 in)
Width around chest	23 cm	(9 in)
Sleeve seam	9 cm	(3½ in)

Skirt

Waist to hem	14 cm	(5½ in)
Width around waist	26 cm	(10¼ in)
Width around hem	42 cm	(16½ in)

Panties

Waist to crutch	12 cm	(4¾ in)
Width around waist	25 cm	(10 in)
Side seam	12.5 cm	(5 in)

Tension

8sts = 2.5 cm (1 in)

Henry's jumper

Front

With 3.25 mm (10) (US 3) needles and MC, cast on 40 sts.
Work 6 rows in k1, p1 rib, inc 1 st at end of 6th row (41 sts).

1st row	Knit MC.
2nd row	Purl MC.
3rd row	Join in W, knit.
4th row	Purl with W.
5th row	Knit: 1W, *1MC, 2W, 1MC, 2W, 1MC, 1W.
6th row	Purl: 1MC, *2W, 3MC, 2W, 1MC.
7th row	Knit: 1W, *1W, 2MC, 1W, 2MC, 2W.
8th row	Purl: 1W, *1W, 2MC, 1W, 2MC, 2W.
9th row	Knit: 1MC, *2W, 3MC, 2W, 1MC.
10th row	Purl: 1W *1MC, 2W, 1MC, 2W, 1MC, 1W.
11th row	Knit W.
12th row	Purl W.

Rep rows 1–8.

Armhole

Continue in pattern as set, cast off 3 sts at beg of next 2 rows.
Next row k2 tog at both ends of row.**
Continuing in pattern, work 6 rows.
Next row p11, cast off 11 sts, p11.
Next row On the last 11 sts, pattern to last 2 sts, k2 tog (neck).

Work 6 rows in pattern. Cast off.
Join in both colours to remaining neck edge.
Working in pattern, k2 tog, knit to end.
Work 6 rows in pattern. Cast off.

Back
With 3.25 mm (10) (US 3) needles and MC, cast on 40 sts
and work in rib as given for front, inc 1 st at end of 6th row.
Work 20 rows in st st.

Armhole
Cast off 3 sts at beg of next 2 rows.
Next row   k2 tog at both ends of row.
Work 13 rows in st st.
Cast off 10 st, work next 13 sts in rib, cast off 10 sts. Break
off wool
Rejoin wool to middle sts, and work 3 rows in k1, p1 rib.
Cast off.

Sleeves
With 3.25 mm (10) (US 3) needles and MC, cast on 27 sts
and work 3 rows in k1, p1 rib.
Next row   *rib 3, inc in next st, rep from * to last 3 sts, rib
3 (33 sts).
Work 28 rows in st st.
Cast off 4 sts at the beg of the next 6 rows.
Cast off remaining sts.
Work another sleeve the same way.

To make up
Working from the armhole edge, sew up corresponding 6 sts
on each shoulder seam. Pick up 26 sts evenly around front
neck. Work 4 rows in k1, p1 rib. Cast off.
Sew sleeves into position in armholes, then sew up sleeve
and side seams.

Henry's trousers (slacks)

Worked from waist down.

Right leg
**With 2.75 mm (12) (US 2) needles and MC, cast on 30 sts
loosely.
Note If a tight knitter-use 3.00 mm (11) (US 2–3) needles
throughout.
1st row   Knit.
2nd row   Purl.
Rep first and 2nd rows once.
5th and 6th rows   Purl.
Rep first and 2nd rows twice.
Next row (Hem)   Fold cast-on edge to back of work, then
with left hand needle, pick up 1 st from cast on edge, and

knit it together with 1 st on left hand needle. Rep process
until all sts have been picked up and knitted together with
sts on left hand needle (30 sts now on right hand needle).
Next row   Purl.
Next row   k4, *inc in next st, k2, rep from * to last 2 sts, k2
(38 sts).
Change to 3.00 mm (11) (US 2–3) needles.
Next row   Purl.**

Shape back
1st row   K10, turn.
2nd row   sl 1, p9.
3rd row   k20, turn.
4th row   sl 1, p19.
5th row   k30, turn.
6th row   sl 1, p29.
Work 2 rows in st st.
*** *Next row*   Inc once at beg of row. Knit to end.
Work 3 rows in st st.
Next row   Knit. Inc once at each end of needle.***
Work 3 rows in st. st.
Rep from *** to *** once (44sts).
Note Work 3 rows in st st for right leg. Work 2 rows in st st
for left leg.

**** *Shaping the leg*
Cast off 2 sts at beg of next 2 rows.
Dec one at each end of needle in next and 2 following alt
rows (34 sts).
Work 5 rows in st st without shaping.
Next row   Dec 1 st at each end of needle.
Rep these last 6 rows 3 times (26 sts).
Work 8 rows for right leg, (7 rows for left leg) or length
required.
Change to 2.75 mm (12) (US 2) needles to work hem.
Work 4 rows in st st.
5th and 6th rows   Purl.
7th row   Knit.
8th row   Purl. Cast off.

Left leg
Work as given for right leg from ** to **.
Next row   Knit.

Shape back
1st row   p10, turn.
2nd row   sl 1, k9.
3rd row   p20, turn.
4th row   sl 1, k19.
5th row   p30, turn.
6th row   sl 1, k29.
Work 2 rows in st st.
Work from *** as per right leg to cast off.

To make up
Sew up back and front seams. Leave slots at waist open to thread elastic through. Turn up hem at purl row. Slip stitch in position.

Henrietta's jumper

Work front of jumper as per instructions given for Henry's jumper.
Work back of jumper, same as front until armhole decreases have been worked.
Work 13 rows in pattern as set.
Next row   With MC, cast off 10 st, rib next 13 st, cast off 10 st.
Rejoin wool to ribbing and work 3 more rows in rib. Cast off.

Sleeves
Work as given for Henry's jumper.

To Make up
Make up exactly as Henry's jumper.

Henrietta's skirt

Worked in one piece.
With 3.25 mm (10) (US 3) needles and MC, cast on 144 sts and work 4 rows in k1, p1 rib.
Working the main part of the skirt in st st proceed as follows:
1st row   *k2 tog, k16, rep from * to end of row.
Work 5 rows in st st.
7th row   *k2 tog, k15, rep from * to end of row.
Work 5 rows in st st.
13th row   *k2 tog, k14, rep from * to end of row.
Work 5 rows in st st.
Continue in this manner, working one st less between decreases in every 6th row, until the 37th row (k2 tog, k10) has been worked.
Work 3 rows in k1, p1 rib.
Elastic holes   *rib 2, m1, k2 tog, rep from * to end.
Work 2 more rows in k1, p1 rib. Cast off in rib.

To make up
Join up seam. Thread elastic through holes at waist.

Henrietta's panties

Worked as one piece.
With 3.25 mm (10) (US 3) needles and W, cast on 40 sts.
Work 2 rows in k1, p1 rib.
Next row   k2, *m1, k2 tog, rep from * to end of row.
Work 3 rows in k1, p1 rib.
Work 5 rows in st st.
Inc one st at each end of the following row, and then every 6th row, 3 times (48 sts).
Work 3 rows in st st.

Gusset shaping
1st row   k23, (k1, p1 into the next st), (p1, k1 into the next st), k23.
2nd and all alternate rows   Purl.
3rd row   k23, (k1, p1 into next st), k2, (p1, k1 into next st), k23.
5th row   k23, (k1, p1 into next st), k4, (p1, k1 into next st), k23.
Continue to inc on every 2nd row, working 2 sts extra between inc until k23, (k1, p1 into next st), k10, (p1, k1 into next sts), k23 has been reached (60 sts).

Leg openings
Purl 1 row. Cast off 25 sts at the end of the next 2 rows.
Cast on 25 sts at the beginning of the next 2 rows.

Gusset decreases
1st row   k23, k2 tog, k10, sl 1, k1, psso, k23.
2nd and alternate rows   Purl.
3rd row   k23, k2 tog, k8, sl 1, k1, psso, k23.
Continue dec in this way till there are 48 sts on the needle.
Work 3 rows in st st.
Dec 1 st at each end of the next row, and in the following 6th rows, until there are 40 sts on the needle.
Work 5 rows in st st.
Work 3 rows in k1, p1 rib.
Next row   k2, *m1, k2 tog, rep from * to end of row.
Work 2 rows in rib. Cast off in rib.

To make up
If you wish, you can crochet around the leg openings or you can pick up and knit 53 sts evenly along each leg opening, knit one row and cast off; or work 3 rows of k1, p1 rib on the 53 sts. Sew up side seams.

Ira and Iris

This lovely duo of outfits, originally designed in the 1940s–50s for the smaller baby dolls of the era, have been adapted to suit dolls of all ages. Using 3-ply yarn, the leggings pattern is used for both the 18–20 cm (7–8 in) boy and girl dolls, but are finished with different jackets and headgear to suit each type of doll. By using 2–ply and smaller needles, the outfits will fit the popular 15 cm (6 in) hard plastic dolls of the 1950s.

Materials

25 g (1 oz) 3-ply wool in MC for Ira's leggings, jacket and cap
25 g (1oz) 3-ply wool in C for Ira's jacket and cap
25 g (1 oz) 3-ply wool in MC for Iris's leggings
25g (1oz) 3-ply wool in C for Iris's jacket and bonnet
1 pair 3.00 mm (11) (US 2–3) knitting needles
1 pair 2.25 mm (13) (US 1) knitting needles
Small buttons or beads (6 for the boys jacket, 4 for the girl's jacket)
Length of fine elastic or ribbon for leggings

Measurements

Ira and Iris

Leggings

Waist to crutch	5.5 cm	(2¼ in)
Width around waist	17 cm	(6¼ in)
Outside leg (waist to toe)	13 cm	(5¼ in)
Inside leg (crutch to toe)	9 cm	(3½ in)

Ira

Jacket

Shoulder to hem	7 cm	(2¾ in)
Width around hem	22 cm	(8½ in)
Width around chest (fastened)	16 cm	(6¼ in)
Sleeve seam	5 cm	(1¾ in)
Beret		
Circumference	16 cm	(6¼ in)
Brim to crown	6 cm	(2¼ in)

Iris

Jacket

Shoulder to hem	7.5 cm	(3 in)
Width around hem	25 cm	(10 in)
Width around chest (fastened)	16 cm	(6¼ in)
Sleeve seam	3.5 cm	(1½ in)
Bonnet		
Around face	13 cm	(5¼ in)
Brim to crown	7 cm	(2¾ in)
Front (after turnback) to back	5.5 cm	(2¼ in)

Tension

8st = 2.5 cm (1 in)

Ira and Iris's leggings

Starting at the waist with 3.00 mm (11) (US 2–3) needles and MC, cast on 32 sts and work 2 rows in k1, p1 rib.
Next row   k2, *m1, k2 tog, rep from * to end of row.
Work 3 rows in k1, p1 rib.
Work 10 rows in st st.
Dec 1 st at each end of row, until 22 sts remain.
Work 15 rows in st st without further shaping (can be lengthened or shortened here).
Change to 2.25 mm (13) (US 1) needles and work 2 rows in k1, p1 rib.
Note: If you don't want to include feet in your leggings, work another 2 rows of k1, p1 rib, then cast off.
Change to 3.00 mm (11) (US 2–3) needles and work foot as follows:
1st row   k22.
2nd row   p2 tog, p7, p2 tog, p2 tog, p7, p2 tog (18sts).
3rd and following alternate rows   Knit.
4th row   p2 tog, p5, p2 tog, p2 tog, p5, p2 tog (14 sts).
6th row   p2 tog, p3, p2 tog, p2 tog, p3, p2 tog (10sts).
7th row   Knit. Cast off.
Make another leg the same.

To make up
Sew up front and back seams, then sew up inside leg seams.

Ira's jacket

Back
With 3.00 mm (11) (US 2–3) needles and C, cast on 28 sts and work in ms as follows.
1st row   *k1, p1, rep from * to end of row.
2nd row   *p1, k1, rep from * to end of row.
Rep the last 2 rows once.
Work 10 rows in st st.

Armhole shaping
Cast off 2 sts at beg of the next 2 rows, then dec 1 st at each end of the next 3 rows (18sts).
Work 7 rows in st st without further shaping. Cast off.

Right front
With 3.00 mm (11) (US 2–3) needles and C, cast on 16 sts and work 4 rows in ms as given for back.
1st row   Work 8 st in ms, knit to end of row.
2nd row   Purl to last 8 sts, work last 8 sts in ms.
Rep the last 2 rows 4 times, then work the first row again.

Armhole shaping
Cast off 2 sts at beg of next row, then dec 1 st at armhole edge on each of the next 2 rows.
Next row   Join in MC, p2 tog, purl to last 8 sts, ms8.
Keeping the ms border as set, work 1 row in MC, 2 rows in C, 2 rows in MC. Break off MC.

Neck Shaping
Using C, cast off 4 sts at beg of next row, then dec 1 st at neck edge of following row.
Work 1 row. Cast off.

Left front
With 3.00 mm (11) (US 2–3) needles and C, cast on 16 sts and work 4 rows in ms.
1st row   Knit to the last 8 sts, ms8.
2nd row   ms8, purl to end of row.
Rep the last 2 rows 4 times.

Armhole shaping
Cast off 2 sts at beg of next row, then dec 1 st at armhole edge on next 3 rows.
Keeping the ms border as set, join in MC, and work 2 rows of MC, 2 rows C, 1 row of MC.

Neck shaping
Cast off 4 sts at beg of next row. Break off MC.
Next row   Using C, dec 1 st at neck edge.
Work 1 row. Cast off.

Sleeves
Worked from the top down.
With 3.00 mm (11) (US 2–3) needles and C, cast on 8 sts.
Knit 1 row.
Beginning with a purl row, continue in st st, but inc 1 st at each end of every row until there are 18 sts on your needle.
Work 12 rows in st st without further shaping.
Work 4 rows in ms. Cast off.
Work another sleeve the same.
Sew up shoulder seams.

Collar
With right side of work facing, join yarn to 5th st from the front edge, and using 3.00 mm (11) (US 2–3) needle and MC, pick up 22 sts around neck, finishing at 5th st from other front edge.
Working in ms, inc 1 st at each end of next, and every following row until there are 32 sts on the needle.
Work 1 row. Cast off loosely.

To make up
Sew sleeves into position, then sew up sleeve and side seams. Place left front over right front, and mark positions for 6 buttons (for a double-breasted effect) or 4 buttons (for single-breasted jacket). Sew tiny buttons or pearl beads in place on right hand side of jacket and gently push through left hand side of jacket to fasten. Fold back cuffs of sleeves if needed.

Ira's beret

With 2.25 mm (13) (US 1) needles and MC, cast on 64 sts.
Work 4 rows in k1, p1 rib.
Change to 3.00 mm (11) (US 2–3) needles and working in st st, work 4 rows in MC, 2 rows in C, 2 rows in MC.
Keeping stripe pattern of 2 rows C, 2 rows MC, shape top of beret as follows:
1st row   *k6, k2 tog, rep from * to end of row.
2nd and all alternate rows   Purl.
3rd row   *k5, k2 tog, rep from * to end of row.
5th row   *k4, k2 tog, rep from * to end of row.
7th row   *k3, k2 tog, rep from * to end of row.
9th row   *k2, k2 tog, rep from * to end of row. Break off wool.
Thread wool through remaining sts. Fasten off securely, then sew up seam.

Iris's jacket

Back
Using 3.00 mm (11) (US 2–3) needles and C, cast on 35 sts.
Work 4 rows in ms.
Work 8 rows in st st.
Next row k1, *k2 tog, k3, rep from * to last 4 sts, k2 tog, k2 (28 sts).
Work 3 rows in ms.
Work 2 rows in st st.

Armhole shaping
Cast off 2 sts at beg of next 2 rows, then dec 1 st at each end of the next 3 rows.
Work 7 rows in st st without further shaping. Cast off.

Right front
With 3.00 mm (11) (US 2–3) needles and C, cast on 20 sts and work 4 rows in ms.
1st row ms4, knit to end of row.
2nd row Purl to last 4 sts, ms4.
Rep last 2 rows 3 times.
Next row ms3, p2 tog, *k3, k2 tog, rep from * to end of row (16 sts).
Work 3 rows of ms.
Work 3 rows in st st.

****Armhole shaping**
Cast off 2 sts at beg of next row, then dec 1 st at armhole edge on next 3 rows.
Work 5 rows in st st, ending at front edge.

Neck shaping
Cast off 4 sts at beginning of row.
Next row Work to last 2 sts, p2 tog.
Work 1 row. Cast off. ***

Left front
With 3.00 mm (11) (US 2–3) needles and C, cast on 20 sts and work 4 rows in ms.
1st row Knit to last 4 sts, ms4
2nd row ms4, purl to end of row.
Rep the last 2 rows 3 times, then first row again.
Next row ms3, k2 tog, *p3, p2tog, rep to last 2 sts, p2 (16sts).
Work 3 rows in ms.
Work 3 rows in st st.
Work armhole shaping etc as right front from *** to ***.

Sleeves
With 3.00 mm (11) (US 2–3) needles and C, cast on 16 st and work 4 rows in ms.
Work 10 rows in st st.

Armhole shaping
Cast off 2 sts at beg of next 2 rows, then dec 1 st at each end of next 4 rows. Cast off.
Join shoulder seams.
Using 3.00 mm (11) (US 2–3) needles, and starting 5 sts in from front edge, pick up and knit 24 sts around neck, finishing on 5th st from other front edge.
Working in ms, inc 1 st at each end of every alternate row, until there are 30 sts on the needle. Cast off loosely.

To make up
Sew in sleeves, sew up sleeve seam and side seam. Place right front over left front and mark where 4 buttons (or pearl beads) are to go on left hand side. Sew on buttons (or beads), and gently poke through knitting to fasten garment.

Iris's bonnet

Using 3.00 mm (11) (US 2–3) needles and C, cast on 40 sts and work 6 rows in ms.
Work 4 rows in k1, p1 rib.
Work 14 rows in st st.
Cast off 14 sts at start of next 2 rows, then working throughout in ms, work 4 rows on remaining 12 sts.
Dec 1 st at each end of next and every following 8th row until 8 sts remain.
Work 5 rows. Cast off.

To make up
Join the cast off edges to sides of back extension, easing in slightly to fit, if necessary.

Julian and Julia

Worked in 4-ply, these two delightful outfits of the 1950s for 33–36 cm (13–14 in) slim-bodied boy and girl dolls, no matter whether they are the lovely old bisque headed dolls of yesterday, hard plastic dolls of the 1950s, or today's modern plastic. Included in the patterns for the two outfits, are a skirt and panties for the girl doll, short trousers and beret for the boy doll and two lovely jumpers worked in a check design. The girl's jumper plus hat uses only two colours, while the boy's jumper, using exactly the same number of stitches etc., incorporates three colours.

Materials

25 g (1 oz) 3-ply wool in MC for Julia's jumper and hat
25 g (1oz) 3-ply wool in C for Julia's skirt
50 g (2 oz) 3-ply wool in W for Julia and Julian's jumper and Julia's hat and panties
50 g (2 oz) 3-ply wool in MC for Julian's pants, jumper and beret
25 g (1 oz) 3-ply wool in C for Julian's jumper
1 pair 3.25 mm (10) (US 2–3) knitting needles
Buttons or snap fasteners for shoulder closing of jumpers

Measurements

Julian

Pants

Waist to crutch	8 cm	(3¼ in)
Width around waist	20 cm	(8 in)
Waist to bottom of leg	10 cm	(4 in)
Inside leg	2 cm	(¾ in)

Jumper

Shoulder to hem	10 cm	(4 in)
Width around chest	18 cm	(7 in)
Side seam	5.5 cm	(2¼ in)
Sleeve seam	5.5 cm	(2¼ in)

Beret

Circumference	28 cm	(11 in)
Brim to crown	7.5 cm	(3 in)

Julia

Jumper

Shoulder to hem	10 cm	(4 in)
Width around chest	18 cm	(7 in)
Side seam	5.5 cm	(2¼ in)
Sleeve seam	5.5 cm	(2¼ in)

Skirt

Waist to hem	9 cm	(3½ in)
Width around waist	18 cm	(7 in)
Width around hem (unstretched)	26 cm	(10¼ in)

Panties

Waist to crutch	7.5 cm	(3 in)
Width around waist	17 cm	(6¼ in)
Side seam	5 cm	(2 in)

Tension

8 sts = 2.5 cm (1 in)

Julian's pants

First leg

Starting at the waist, with 3.25 mm (10) (US 3) needles and MC, cast on 32 sts.
Work 4 rows in k1, p1 rib.
Work 26 rows in st st, placing a coloured length of wool as a marker at each end of the 23rd row.
Work 6 rows in k1, p1 rib. Cast off in rib.
Work a second leg the same.

To make up

Sew up front and back seams to coloured markers. Sew up leg seams to coloured markers.
If needed, thread narrow elastic through ribbing at waist.

Julian's jumper

Note Sleeves are worked as part of the front and back.

Front

** With 3.25 mm (10) (US 3) needles and MC, cast on 34 sts.
Work 4 rows in k1, p1 rib.

Check pattern

MC = main colour, C = contrast, W = white
1st row   *k2 MC, k2 W, rep from * to last 2 sts, k2 MC.
2nd row   *p2 MC, p2 W, rep from * to last 2 sts, p2 MC.
3rd row   *k2 W, k2 C, rep from * to last 2 sts, k2 W.

4th row   *p2 W, p2 C, rep from * to last 2 sts, p2 W.
Rep the last 4 rows twice.

Sleeve shaping

Keep the pattern as set.
Cast on 15 sts, pattern across 34 sts, cast on 15 sts.
Continue in pattern until 10 rows have been worked since start of sleeves**.

Neck and shoulder shaping

Cast off 15 sts, work 11 sts in pattern, cast off 10 sts, work 11 sts in pattern, cast off 15 sts.
Rejoin wool to last 11 sts, work 9 sts in pattern, p2 tog.
Work 2 rows in pattern. Cast off.
Rejoin wool to 2nd half of front, p2 tog, purl to end.
Work 2 rows in pattern. Cast off.

Back

Work as for Front from ** to **.

Shoulder shaping

Cast off 15 sts, work in pattern to last 15 sts. Cast off 15 sts.
Rejoin wool to remaining 34 sts, work 2 rows in pattern.
Cast off 8 sts at beginning of next 2 rows. Cast off remaining sts.

To make up

Pick up 26 sts around front neck. Work 3 rows in k1, p1 rib. Cast off.
Pick up 22 sts along back neck. Work 3 rows in k1, p1 rib. Cast off.
Sew up sleeve seams to shoulder. Sew up underarm seams and side seams. Work 2 rows of dc (US sc) along each back shoulder. Work 1 row of dc (US sc) plus 2 loops (for buttonholes) along each front shoulder. Close with 2 buttons on each side. Or you can omit the dc (US sc) and just close shoulder openings with snap fasteners.

Julian's beret

With 3.25 mm (10) (US 3) needles in MC, cast on 74 sts.
Work 4 rows in k1, p1 rib, inc 1 st at end of last row.
Next row   *k1, inc in next st, rep from * to end (112 sts).
Next row   *k1, p2 tog, purl to last st, k1.
Work 4 rows in st st.
1st row   *k9, k2 tog, rep from * to end of row.
2nd and each alternate row   Purl.
3rd row   *k8, k2 tog, rep from * to end of row.
5th row   *k7, k2 tog, rep from * to end of row.
7th row   *k6, k2 tog, rep from * to end of row.
Continue dec in this way, until *k2, k2 tog row has been worked. Break off wool.
Thread wool double in a darning needle and thread through remaining sts, draw up all sts, and end off securely. Sew up seam.

Julia's jumper

Front and back

Work as per Julian's jumper, but working the 4 pattern rows as follows:
1st row   *k2 MC, k2 W, rep from * to last 2 sts, k2 MC.
2nd row   *p2 MC, p2 W, rep from * to last 2 sts, p2 MC.
3rd row   *k2 W, k2 MC, rep from * to last 2 sts, k2 W.
4th row   *p2 W, p2 MC, rep from * to last 2 sts, k2 MC.

To make up

Join right shoulder seam. Pick up 42 sts evenly around neck and knit. Work 3 rows in k1, p1 rib. Cast off loosely. Sew up the 15 sts of left shoulder. Work 1 row of dc (US sc) on each side of remaining part of left shoulder. Fasten shoulder with snap fasteners.

Julia's skirt

Front and back

With 3.25 mm (10) (US 3) needles and C, cast on 117sts.
1st row   *k4, (p1, k1 3 times), p3, rep from * to end of row
2nd row   *k3 (p1, k1 3 times) p4, rep from * to end of row.
These 2 rows form the pattern.
Rep these 2 rows 11 times, then the first row again.
Next row   *k2, work 3 tog, rep from * to last st, p1 (41 sts).
Work 10 rows in st st.

To make up

Join side seams. Fold over waistband and carefully stitch down on wrong side, leaving an opening to thread elastic through.

Julia's panties

With 3.25 mm (10) (US 3) needles and W, cast on 29 sts.
Work 4 rows in k1, p1 rib.
Work 12 rows in st st.

Shape leg openings

Dec 1 st at both ends of every row until 7 sts remain. Cast off.
Work another piece the same.

To make up

Join up side seams, and cast off seams. If necessary run thin elastic through ribbing at waist.

Julia's hat

With 3.25 mm (10) (US 3) needles and MC, cast on 74 sts.
Work 8 rows in k1, p1 rib.
Work the 4 rows of pattern, as given for jumper, 5 times.
Break off wool, and using thread double, thread through all stitches on needle. Draw up stitches tightly and fasten off securely. If you wish, make a two coloured pom-pom for top of hat.

Kim and Kimberley

Originally published in the 1930s, these outfits are suitable for dolls, of all types and ages, in the 36–41cm (14–16 in) size range. Quick and easy to knit, they consist of a jumper and short pants for a boy doll and dress and panties for a girl doll. A matching design is repeated in the boy doll's jumper and the skirt of the girl doll's dress.

Materials

50 g (2 oz) 3-ply wool for Kimberley's dress and panties
25 g (1 oz) 3-ply wool for Kim's jumper
25 g (1 oz) 3-ply wool for Kim's short pants
1 pair 3.00 mm (11) (US 2–3) knitting needles
1 pair 3.25 (10) (US 3) knitting needles
1 pair 3.75 mm (9) (US 5) knitting needles
4 buttons (2 for Kimberley's dress, 2 for Kim's jumper)
Length of narrow elastic for pants

Measurements

Kim

Jumper

Shoulder to hem	14 cm	(5½ in)
Width around chest	30 cm	(12 in)
Side seam	7 cm	(2¾ in)
Sleeve seam	9.5 cm	(3¾ in)

Short pants

Waist to crutch (back)	12 cm	(4¾ in)
Waist to crutch (front)	9.5 cm	(3¾ in)
Width around waist	24 cm	(9½ in)
Side seam	14 cm	(5½ in)
Inside leg seam	4 cm	(1½ in)

Kimberley

Dress

Shoulder to hem	21 cm	(8¼ in)
Shoulder to waist	9 cm	(3½ in)
Width around chest	28 cm	(11 in)
Width around hem	46 cm	(18 in)
Sleeve seam	5 cm	(2 in)

Panties

Waist to crutch (back)	13 cm	(5 in)
Waist to crutch (front)	12 cm	(4¾ in)
Side seam	9.5 cm	(3¾ in)

Tension

7 sts = 2.5 cm (1 in)

Kim's jumper

Front

With 3.00 mm (11) (US 2–3) needles, cast on 42 sts.
Work 8 rows in k1, p1 rib.
Change to 3.75 mm (9) (US 5) needles and work as follows:

1st row   Knit.
2nd row   Purl.
3rd row   k16, (p2, k2 twice), p2, k16.
4th row   p16, (k2, p2 twice), k2, p16.
5th row   k18, p2, k2, p2, k18.
6th row   p18, k2, p2, k2, p18.
7th row   k20, p2, k20.
8th row   p20, k2, p20.
Rep the first and 2nd rows 5 times.

***Armhole shaping and divide for front opening**
1st row   Cast off 3 sts, knit to end.
2nd row   Cast off 3 sts, p17 (18 sts on right hand needle), turn and work 8 rows in st st.

Neck shaping
Next row   Cast off 4 sts at beg of row.
Work 8 rows of st st. Cast off.
Rejoin wool to remaining 18 sts and work left side of front to match the right side.**

Back
With 3.00 mm (11) (US 2–3) needles, cast on 42 sts.
Work 8 rows in k1, p1 rib.
Work 18 rows in st st.

Armhole shaping
Cast off 3 sts at beg of next 2 rows.
Work 20 rows in st st. Cast off.

Sleeves
Worked from top down.
With 3.75 mm (9) (US 5) needles, cast on 44 sts.
1st row   Knit.

2nd row   Purl.
3rd row   k2 tog, knit to last 2 sts, k2 tog.
4th row   Purl.
5th row   Knit.
6th row   p2 tog, purl to last 2 sts, p2 tog.
Rep the last 6 rows twice, then rep rows 1–3 inclusive (30 sts).
Work 3 rows in st st starting with a purl row.
Change to 3.25 mm (10) (US 3) needles, and work 6 rows in k1, p1 rib. Cast off
Work another sleeve the same.

Collar
With 3.75 mm (9) (US 5) needles, cast on 60 sts.
1st row   *k1, p1, rep from * to end of row.
Continue in rib, dec 1 st at both ends of every row, until 48 sts remain. Cast off.

To make up
Sew up shoulder seams. Sew sleeves into armholes. Sew the cast-off edge of collar around the neck, commencing and finishing at the front edge opening. Sew up side and sleeve seams. Attach either 1 or 2 small buttons to one side of front opening and work corresponding loops on the other side of opening.

Kim's pants

Right and Left leg
Starting from waist.
With 3.00 mm (11) (US 2–3) needles, cast on 40 sts.
Work 8 rows in k1, p1 rib.
Change to 3.75 mm (9) (US 5) needles and work as follows:

Right leg (waist shaping)	*Left leg (waist shaping)*
1st row Purl.	*1st row* p8, turn.
2nd row k8, turn.	*2nd row* k8.
3rd row p8.	*3rd row* p16, turn.
4th row k16, turn.	*4th row* k16.
5th row p16.	*5th row* p24, turn.
6th row k24, turn.	*6th row* p24.
7th row p24.	*7th row* p32, turn.
8th row k32, turn.	*8th row* k32.
9th row p32.	*9th row* Purl all 40 sts.

Right leg only
Working in st st, inc 1 st at beg of next row, and every following 4th row, until 5 inc have been worked (45 sts).
*Work 3 rows in st st.
Dec 1 st at both ends of the next row, and every alt row twice (39 sts).
Next row   k1, *p1, k1, rep from * to end.
Next row   p1, *k1, p1 rep from * to end.
Rep the last 2 rows twice. Cast off.*

Left leg
After working the 9 rows of shaping at waist, inc 1 st at end of the next row, and every following 4th row, until 5 inc have been worked (45 sts).
Work as from * to * on right leg to finish off.

To make up
Sew the leg seams, then the back and front seams. Thread narrow elastic through ribbing at waist.

Kimberley's dress

Front
With 3.75 mm (9) (US 5) needles, cast on 63 sts.
Work 4 rows in garter stitch.
1st row   Knit.
2nd row   Purl.
Rep these 2 rows once.
5th row   k10, (p2, k2 4 times), p2, k7, (p2, k2 4 times), p2, k10.
6th row   p10, (k2, p2 4 times), k2, p7, (k2, p2 4 times), k2, p10.
7th row   k12, (p2, k2 3 times), p2, k11, (p2, k2 3 times), p2, k12.
8th row   p12, (k2, p2 3 times), k2, p11, (k2, p2 3 times), k2, p12.
9th row   k14, (p2, k2 twice), p2, k15, (p2, k2 twice), p2, k14.
10th row   p14, (k2, p2 twice), k2, p15, (k2, p2 twice), k2, p14.
11th row   k16, p2, k2, p2, k19, p2, k2, p2, k16.
12th row   p16, k2, p2, k2, p19, k2, p2, k2, p16.
13th row   k18, p2, k23, p2, k18.
14th row   p18, k2, k23, k2, p18.
15th row   Knit.
16th row   Purl.
Rep 15th and 16th rows 10 times.
Change to 3.00 mm (11) (US 2–3) needles.
Next row   *k1, p2 tog, rep from * to end of row (42 sts).
Next row   *k1, p1, rep from * to end.
Rep the last row 4 times.
Change to 3.75 mm (9) (US 5) needles and work 8 rows in st st. Finish with a purl row.

Shape armholes and divide for front opening
Work as given for Front of Kim's jumper.

Back
Work exactly as for Front, to the beginning of the armhole shaping.

Armhole shaping
Cast off 3 sts at the beg of the next 2 rows.
Work 20 rows in st st. Cast off.

Sleeves
Using 3.75 mm (9) (US 5) needles, cast on 44 sts.
Work the first 6 rows as given for Kim's jumper, then work rows 1-4 inclusive again,
Change to 3.25 mm (10) (US 3) needles and work 6 rows in k1, p1 rib.

Collar
Work as given for Kim's jumper.

To make up
Sew up shoulder seams. Sew sleeves into armholes, sew cast-off edge of collar around neck, commencing and finishing at front edge opening. Sew up side and sleeve seams. Attach a fancy button at neck, and a matching loop on other side.

Kimberley's panties

Worked in one piece.
With 3.00 mm (11) (US 2–3) needles, cast on 40 sts.
Work 8 rows in k1, p1 rib.
Change to 3.75 mm (9) (US 5) needles and work as follows:
1st row   Purl.
2nd row   k24, turn.
3rd row   p8, turn.

4th row   k16, turn.
5th row   p24, turn.
6th row   k32, turn.
7th row   Purl to end.
Increase as follows:
1st row   Knit, inc in first and last sts.
2nd and 4th row   Purl.
3rd row   Knit.
Rep the last 4 rows 3 times, then rep the first and 2nd rows once (50 sts).
Working in st st dec 1 st at both ends of every row until 24 sts remain.
Inc 1 st at both ends of every following row until there are 50 sts.
Work 3 rows in st st.
Dec 1 st at both ends of the next and every following 4th row until 40 sts remain.
Change to 3.00 mm (11) (US 2–3) needles and work 8 rows in k1, p1 rib. Cast off.
Using 3.75 mm (9) (US 5) needles pick up and knit 28 sts along one shaped edge of leg and work 8 rows in k1, p1 rib. Cast off. Work the same on other leg opening.

To make up
Sew up side seams and thread a length of narrow elastic or ribbon through waist ribbing and, if you wish, also through leg ribbing.

Lesley and Leslie

Worked throughout in 5-ply, and decorated with a simple 2-row twist stitch, this lovely set was adapted from a 1967 pattern. The outfits, a long-sleeved jumper and short pants for a boy doll and a short-sleeved jumper, skirt and panties for a girl doll are quick to knit and suitable for the popular straight-legged or bent-limbed 36–41 cm (14–16 in) dolls of yesterday and today.

Materials
25 g (1 oz) 5-ply wool for Lesley's jumper
25 g (1 oz) 5-ply wool for Lesley's skirt
25 g (1oz) 5-ply wool for Leslie's jumper
25 g (1oz) 5-ply wool for Leslie's pants
1 pair 3.75 mm (9) (US 5) knitting needles
1 pair 3.00 mm (11) (US 2–3) knitting needles

Measurements

Lesley

Jumper		
Shoulder to hem	14 cm	(5½ in)
Width around chest	26 cm	(10¼ in)
Side seam	7 cm	(2¾ in)
Sleeve seam	3.5 cm	(1½ in)
Skirt		
Waist to hem	11 cm	(4½ in)
Width around waist	26 cm	(10¼ in)
Width around hem	40 cm	(16 in)
Length of shoulder straps	22 cm	(8½ in)

Leslie

Jumper		
Shoulder to hem	14 cm	(5½ in)
Width around chest	26 cm	(10¼ in)
Side seam	7 cm	(2¾ in)
Sleeve seam	8 cm	(3 in)
Pants		
Waist to crutch	11 cm	(4½ in)
Width around waist	25 cm	(10 in)
Side seam	12.5 cm	(5 in)
Inside leg seam	2.5 cm	(1 in)
Shoulder strap	19 cm	(7½ in)

Tension
7 st = 2.5 cm (1 in)

Abbreviation
tw2 = knit into front of 2nd st, then front of first st on left-hand needle, and slip both sts off needle together.

Lesley's jumper

Front
With 3.00 mm (11) (US 2–3) needles, cast on 34 sts.
Work 6 rows in k1, p1 rib.
Change to 3.75 mm (9) (US 5) needles.
1st row k9, p1, *tw2, p1, rep from * 4 times, k9.
2nd row Purl.
Rep the last 2 rows 7 times.
***Keeping the pattern as set, shape raglan armholes as follows:
1st row Cast off 2 st, work in pattern as set to end.
2nd row Cast off 2 sts, purl to end of row.
3rd row k1, k2 tog tbl, work in pattern to last 3 sts, k2 tog, k1.
4th row k1, purl to last st, k1.
5th row Work in pattern.
6th row As 4th row.
Rep rows 3–6 twice (24 sts).

Neck shaping
Next row k1, k2 tog tbl, pattern 5 sts. Cast off 8sts, pattern 5 sts, k2 tog, k1.
On last 7 sts, work as follows:
Dec 1 st at armhole edge (as before) in every alt row twice, whilst at the same time dec 1 st at neck edge in every alt row twice (3 sts).
Dec 1 st at armhole edge only in every alt row until 1 st remains. Fasten off.
Rejoin wool to neck edge of other 7 sts and work to correspond.***

Back

With 3.mm (11) (US 2–3) needles, cast on 34 sts.
Work 6 rows in k1, p1 rib.
Change to 3.75 mm (9) (US 5) needles and work 16 rows
in st st.

Shape raglan armhole and divide for back opening
1st row   Cast off 2 sts, k17, turn.
2nd row   k1, purl to last st, k1.
3rd row   k1, k2 tog tbl, knit to end.
4th row   As 2nd row.
5th row   Knit.
Rep rows 2–5 once, then rows 2–4 once.
13th row—Knit to last 3 sts, m1, k2 tog (buttonhole), k1.
Rep 2nd and 3rd rows 5 times (9 sts). Cast off.
Join in wool at centre back and cast on 4 sts for underlap.
1st row   Knit.
2nd row   Cast off 2 sts, purl to last 4 sts, k4.
3rd row   Knit to last 3 sts, k2 tog, k1.
4th row   k1, purl to last 4 sts, k4.
5th row   Knit.
6th row   As 4th row.
Rep rows 3–6 twice, then 3rd and 4th rows 4 times, then 3rd
row once (9 sts). Cast off.

Sleeves

With 3.00 mm (11) (US 2–3) needles, cast on 25 sts.
Work 4 rows in k1, p1 rib
Change to 3.75 mm (9) (US 5) needles and working in st st.
1st row   *k3, inc, rep from * to last st, k1 (31 sts).
Purl 1 row.
Work 2 rows in st st.
Shape raglan top by working in st st and working rows 1–4
inclusive of raglan shaping on front, then rep 3rd and 4th
rows until 5 sts remain. Cast off.

To make up

Sew sleeves into position. With right side of work facing
and using 3.00 mm (11) (US 2–3) needles pick up and knit
45 sts around neck.
1st row   k4, *p1, k1, rep from * to last 3 sts, k3.
2nd row   k5, *p1, k1, rep from * to last 4 sts, k1, m1, k2 tog
(buttonhole), k1.
Rep first and 2nd rows once, omitting buttonhole. Cast off
loosely in rib.
Sew underlap in position, sew up side seams. Sew on
buttons to match buttonholes.

Lesley's skirt

Back and front

With 3.75 mm (9) (US 5), cast on 52 sts.
1st row   *p1, tw2, rep from * to last st, p1.
2nd row   Purl.

Rep last 2 rows 4 times.
1st row   k12, p1, tw2, p1, k8, p1, tw2, p1, k8, p1, tw2, p1,
k12.
2nd row   Purl.
Rep the last 2 rows 4 times
1st row   k10, k2 tog, p1, tw2, p1, k2 tog, k4, k2 tog, p1,
tw2, p1, k2 tog, k4, k2 tog, p1, tw2, p1, k2 tog, k10 (46 sts).
2nd row   Purl.
3rd row   k11, p1, tw2, p1, k6, p1, tw2, p1, k6, p1, tw2, p1,
k11.
4th row   Purl.
Rep the last 2 rows twice.
Next row   k2 tog, k1, *k2tog, k3 rep from * 8 times, k1, k2
tog (36sts).
Change to 3.00 mm (11) (US 2–3) needles and work 6 rows
in k1, p1 rib. Cast off loosely in rib.

Shoulder straps

With 3.00 mm (11) (US 2–3) needles, cast on 8 sts.
1st row   k2, p1, tw2, p1, k2.
2nd row   Purl.
Rep these 2 rows 31 times. Cast off.

To make up

Sew up side seams, sew straps into position at front (top of
the two outer twist patterns), and cross over at centre twist
pattern at back and secure firmly.

Leslie's jumper

Front

With 3.00 mm (11) (US 2–3) needles, cast on 34 sts.
Work 6 rows in k1, p1 rib.
Change to 3.75 mm (9) (US 5) needles and work in pattern
as follows:
1st row   k9, p1, *tw2, p1, k2, p1, tw2, p1, k2, p1, tw2, p1,
k9.
2nd row   Purl.
Rep the last 2 rows 7 times.
Work from *** to *** on Lesley's jumper.

Back

Work same as Lesley's jumper.

Sleeves

With 3.00 mm (11) (US 2–3) needles, cast on 25 sts.
Work 6 rows in k1, p1 rib.
Change to 3.75 mm (9) (US 5) needles and working in st st,
inc 1 st at both ends of next and every following 6th row,
twice (31 sts).
Work 5 rows in st st starting with a purl row.
Shape raglan top by working rows 1–4 inclusive of raglan
shaping on jumper front, then rep 3rd and 4th rows until
4 sts remain. Cast off.

To make up
Make up exactly as given for Lesley's jumper.

Leslie's short pants

Right leg
Working from bottom to top.
With 3.00 mm (11) (US 2–3) needles, cast on 44 sts and work 8 rows in k1, p1 rib.
Change to 3.75 mm (9) (US 5) needles as work as follows:
1st row   k8, (p1, tw2) twice, p1, k14, (p1, tw2) twice, p1, k8.
2nd row   Purl.
Keeping pattern correct, inc 1 st at each end of next 2 rows (48 sts). Place a marker thread at each end of row.
Keeping pattern as set, dec 1 st at both ends of next and every alt row until 40 sts remain, then in every 4th row until 36 sts remain. **
Keeping front edge straight, dec 1 st at end only of following 4th row.
Work 6 rows in pattern.

Shape back as follows
1st row   Work across 14 sts, turn.
2nd row   Work to end.
3rd row   Work across 7 sts, turn.
4th row   As 2nd row.
5th row   Work across all sts.
Change to 3.00 mm (11) (US 2–3) needles and work 6 rows in k1, p1 rib. Cast off loosely in rib.

Left leg
Work as right leg to **.
Keeping front edge straight, dec 1 st at beg of following 4th row.
Work 7 rows in pattern.
1st row   Work across 14 sts, turn.
2nd row   Work to end.
3rd row   Work across 7 sts, turn.
4th row   As 2nd row.
Change to 3.00 mm (11) (US 2–3) needles and work 6 rows in k1, p1 rib. Cast off.

Straps
With 3.00 mm (11) (US 2–3) needles, cast on 8 sts.
1st row   k2, p1, tw2, p1, k2.
2nd row   p2, k1, p2, k1, p1.
Rep the last two row 29 times. Cast off.

To make up
Sew back and front seams from waist to coloured markers. Sew up leg seams. Attach straps to waist at front, corresponding with fancy pattern and cross over, and attach to back seam.

Suppliers

Look in your local phone book under the Craft section if no other classification seems appropriate.

Coats Patons wool is available in most shops specialising in knitting yarns, and also in the haberdashery departments of large stores such as Myers, David Jones, Big W, Spotlight and K-Mart.

You may find also wools from England in the 2-ply, 3-ply and 4-ply range in many of the specialised wool shops in the southern states of Australia and overseas. Finer wools such as 1-ply can be obtained from miniature (dollhouse) outlets.

Bendigo Woollen Mills offer a speedy mail-order service to their customers, and take most major credit cards. They will willingly send you a sample card of their wools and the colours available for each ply.

Australia
Bendigo Woollen Mills
Lansell Street,
Bendigo, Vic. 3550
Phone (03) 5442 4600
Fax (03) 5442 2918

Champion Textiles
16–18 O'Connell Street
Newtown, NSW 2042
Phone (02) 9519 6677
Toll free 1800 672 831
Fax (02) 9510 9605

Miniature Design Co
PO Box 438
Woodridge, Qld 4114
Phone (07) 3209 5672
For fine knitting needles sizes 14–20 and 1-ply wool in all shades, also 1-ply nylon, crepe and mohair. Mail orders accepted.

United States
Bendigo Woollen Mills
Toll free 1 888 235 1993
Fax + 613 5442 2918

Index